I0029324

*An Approach to*
PUBLIC WELFARE AND SOCIAL WORK

# THE UNIVERSITY OF NORTH CAROLINA
## SOCIAL STUDY SERIES

*An Approach to*

# PUBLIC WELFARE AND SOCIAL WORK

BY

## HOWARD W. ODUM, PH.D.

*Kenan Professor of Sociology and Director of the
School of Public Welfare, University
of North Carolina*

CHAPEL HILL

THE UNIVERSITY OF NORTH CAROLINA PRESS

LONDON: HUMPHREY MILFORD

OXFORD UNIVERSITY PRESS

**1926**

*To the County Superintendents
of Public Welfare in
North Carolina*

# CONTENTS

periments    in    Community    Organization—
Theories and Principles of Community Organization—Special Questions for Study and Illustration—The County as a Unit of Social Work—
The City Department of Public Welfare.

## CHAPTER VIII

An Example of Analysis—The North Carolina
Plan   of   Public   Welfare—Special   Difficul-
ties—Seven   Years   of   Experiment—Marked
Limitations—Promising Features—A Mountain
County—Other   Types—The   Outlook—Study
and  Research—Fifteen  Type  Studies—Social
Work  and  Experiment—Training  for  Social
Work—The Larger Program.

## CHAPTER IX

The Problem City as a Review and Summary—
The New City—Varied Problems of Social Relationships—Problems of Conflict—Of Direct and
Indirect Importance—The Scope of Problems to
be Met—Remedial and Curative Efforts—Dependent Folks—Dependent Children—Dependent  Aged  and  Infirm—Broken  Homes—
Homeless  and  Workless  Folk—Delinquent

# PREFACE

This outline for the study of Social Problems and Social Relationships is the second in a series of studies of public welfare, of which the first was *Systems of Public Welfare*, published in 1925. The present little volume was first planned as a continuation course for North Carolina County Superintendents of Public Welfare, following their annual short summer institutes held at the University of North Carolina. The manuscript and general plan of the manual were, therefore, submitted to them and approved at their 1926 Summer session.

It was then suggested by them and others that such a course, dealing with social problems and approaching the subject from the viewpoint of public welfare and social work, ought to be extended to include many teachers who wish correspondence courses in the field of social study. It was suggested further that such a course ought to be included in every college so that students might not only become versed in the essentials of social study, but that they might go back into their communities with a sympathetic understanding of public welfare and social work. The volume has been arranged with these purposes in view, and is offered also to other study groups, such as extension university classes, women's clubs, and library reading groups.

Chapters VIII and IX are offered as an approach to one of the most timely and difficult problems in the fields of social work and government. It is the problem of governmental responsibility for social work and the consequent adjustment of the relation between public welfare and voluntary social work. The results of comprehensive studies of this larger problem will be presented subsequently. In the meantime, however, it is hoped that these preliminary chapters may have the critical examination of specialists in these fields.

From the preliminary enthusiasm with which the plan and volume have been received it seems probable that the outline will meet a very definite need. It should be remembered, however, that it is only an outline and an approach to social work and public welfare through the study of social problems and social relationships. The plan of study conforms to the current tendency of teachers to utilize outlines freely in class, and to require other readings more generously than in the old plan of a single textbook.

For use in college classes the outline provides that the library furnish several copies of each reference book. For the use of extension classes and correspondence courses of various kinds most University Libraries or Extension Divisions will usually arrange to lend copies or provide them at cost. In order to facilitate the work for correspondence courses, and to offer a uniform basis for comparison of work done by different groups of students and in various places, a simple outline of assignments of questions and illustrations is included at the end of the volume.

Although the "approach" as outlined in this volume is elementary, it is clear from an examination of the text that it may also be made quite comprehensive. It should not therefore be completed with undue haste. For the correspondence student the course should extend over at least the normal school year and include no less than thirty-two assignments. For the college class or university extension work the volume should provide for a full "course." Naturally, sixteen of the assignments may be counted toward a half course if satisfactorily completed according to requirements. Advanced work can be added if desired. Likewise, parts may be omitted to meet the special needs of particular groups, so that it can be made as simple and elementary as the occasion may demand. The volume, too, in many instances, will be used with no thought of college credit.

Coöperation in making the plan adaptable to the purposes stated has been generous. Mrs. Kate Burr Johnson, Commissioner of Public Welfare for North Carolina, and Miss Mary Frances Camp of the Bureau of County Organization have helped with suggestions and endorsement. Dr. P. H. Fleming, Mrs. W. B. Waddill, and Mr. W. E. Stanley, the committee from the North Carolina Association of County Superintendents of Public Welfare, presented the plan to their association for approval. Mr. Roy M. Brown of the University of North Carolina read the manuscript. Mrs. Bertha Wailes of Sweet Briar College, Virginia, contributed the questions in Chapters III, IV, V, and VII, read the preliminary outlines, and also the proofs, for all of which special appreciation is expressed.

H. W. O.

CHAPEL HILL,
July 20, 1926.

*An Approach to*
PUBLIC WELFARE AND SOCIAL WORK

# CHAPTER I

## PUBLIC WELFARE AND SOCIAL WORK

*The Development of Public Welfare.* A keynote
of the modern social trend is undoubtedly the
larger emphasis being placed upon public welfare.
As an integral part of government and of social
work it is receiving more recognition and more
sympathetic study. Not only the social worker,
but also the student and teacher of government,
the publicist and the citizen taxpayer, the philan-
thropist and the educator are all deeply concerned
with the increasing scope and efficiency of public
welfare methods and policies. Likewise, hundreds
of municipalities and counties, the several states
and regions in the United States, and the national
government are seeking ways of making this part
of government more effective and more satisfying
to the general public. The viewpoint of this
approach is that while much progress has been
made since the days of the ideas and practices of
the old charities and corrections scarcely more
than a beginning has as yet really been made.
Incompleteness, uncertainty, inefficiency, indefi-
niteness, and temporary failures are in abundant

3

evidence throughout the whole field of public welfare. There is, furthermore, abundant evidence to show that national and local voluntary social work agencies have failed to comprehend fully, and to incorporate into their methods, many of the fundamentals of public welfare. The story of lack of coöperation and misunderstanding between governmental agencies and private agencies is one which should be rapidly rewritten and the beginning should not be postponed. Consequently, there is this new need, this new interest, and greater enthusiasm for more study and better work in the field of public welfare.

*Public Welfare and Social Work.* In this volume public welfare is interpreted as the social work part of government.[1] This, of course, may refer to municipal government, to county government, to state government, to national government, or to international aspects of the whole field of governmental responsibility for social work. Public welfare, therefore, is a special division and

[1] In Chapters IX and X the scope and meaning of public welfare are illustrated through concrete situations, while in Chapter IX a brief analysis of type problems will be found. Other definitions and principles underlying public welfare may be found in *Systems of Public Welfare* by Howard W. Odum and D. W. Willard.

integral part of the whole field of social work, and must needs bring to bear upon its organization and problems all the science, skill, and craftsmanship which the technique of social work may contribute. What, then, are the objectives of social work? What are its fields? What are its main divisions? Through what specialisms and technical training does it perfect its work? To what extent can the general principles and practices of social work be applied to the field of public welfare? The answers to these and other questions offer important approaches to the whole field of public welfare and social work.

*A Process of Finding the Lost.* There are, of course, many ways of defining social work in terms of both scope and function. One of the best analogical statements would be to refer to social work as a process of finding, restoring and developing the lost in the world of human relationships. This, in other words, is a process or means of social adjustment, or of bringing individuals and institutions back to their normal social relationships. We immediately think of lost individuals needing adjustment to family and society; of lost groups needing adjustment in the social organization; of lost institutions struggling to find themselves in the new order; and of lost truth waiting to be found and to make us free.   In terms of Miss Richmond's classification, it will readily be seen that the fields of social work here refer to our *social case work*, or the process of adjusting the individual to his family and society, *community organization*, or the process of group adjustment and development in society, *social reform*, or the process of adjusting social institutions to meet the great demand of social change, and *social research*, or the process of discovering and adjusting truth to the direction of social relationships.   Public welfare itself might be called the lost process of government, or the process of adjusting government to private, community, civic, and social activities.   Thus, the whole concept of social work takes on the aspect of an age-long search of adjustment and development of the individual in the midst of social institutions.   The task of finding the lost has always been an important one, and one which has appealed to the imagination of humanity.   That social work may use scientific methods in this process does not detract from, but rather adds to, the importance of the new social humanism.

*Tufts' Divisions*.   Professor Tufts defines the

field of social work by referring to five phases.
One is the field of aiding certain disadvantaged
classes, such as the poor, ill, defective, perverse, or
otherwise handicapped. His second definition
refers to social work as a better adjusting of
social relations in the world where the social
process is so imperfectly coördinated that certain
individuals or groups are always finding themselves out of adjustment. His third definition
takes into consideration the historical approach
through which society has advanced in scientific
attitude towards causes, scientific methods, and
social control in the treatment of increasingly
larger numbers of disadvantaged folk. He dis-
cusses a fourth definition in terms of fields of
activity of social work, giving eleven phases of
social case work, one-half dozen of social group
work, one-half dozen with reference to social
reform, four each of social research and industrial
social work, and a baker's dozen or more of
"specialists." We should be inclined to emphasize a number of other larger phases, such as
public welfare, psychiatric social work, rural
social work, industrial social work, urban social
work, hospital social work, child welfare, family
case work, and community organization. His

fifth definition is in terms of the relation of social work to social institutions, such as the family, the school, the church, government, industry, community, and the like.

*The National Conference of Social Work.*   One of the best illustrations of the field and scope of social work will be found in the associations, organizations, and groups represented at the National Conference of Social Work each year. For instance, at the 1926 53rd annual meeting at Cleveland there were more than a score of social-work organizations represented, and they dealt with scores of topics of social work.   Among the associations represented were The American Association of Social Workers, The Child Welfare League of America, The American Association for Community Organization, The American Association for Organizing Family Social Work, The American Country Life Association, The National Visiting Teachers Association, The American Association of Hospital Social Workers, The American Association of Schools of Professional Social Work, The National Association of Travellers' Aid Societies, The American Red Cross, The National Federation of Day Nurseries, The National Tuberculosis Association, The Jewish

Social Service Bureau, The Girls Protective Council, and others.   Among the many subjects which they discussed were: child dependency, public health in the federal government, problems of the handicapped, various aspects of the family, various aspects of the community in relation to the family, various aspects of immigration problems, community problems, compulsory education, leadership in social work, religious life, personality, children's agencies, mothers' pensions, child study, juvenile delinquency, and many others.   Thus the 4,000 members present, attacking various aspects of social work, become a national force of great importance.   The fact that they recognize the complexity and difficulties of their problems and the limitations of their methods is hopeful indication that professional social work may achieve its rightful place in the field of the larger professions.

*Twelve Divisions of Work.*   The National Conference in its organization and programs recognizes officially twelve divisions of its work.   These are:

*Division*
   I. Children
   II. Delinquents and Correction
   III. Health

*Other Definitions.*   Important facts and considerations in the several endeavors of social work
to cope with social problems will be discussed in
subsequent chapters in this little volume.   It is
important in this first chapter only to come to
some relative, definite, and simple understanding
of the meaning, scope, and methods of social
work with special reference to the later consideration of public welfare, and the study of social
problems.   Professor Queen in his *Social Work in
the Light of History*, like many others, finds it
difficult to give a clear-cut definition of social work.
Although assuming that such a definition ought to
be easy, he explains that "as a matter of fact, the
field of social service includes so many and so
varied activities, that the answer to the question,
'What is social work?' is a difficult one."   He

concludes that, "Perhaps the nearest we can come to a definition is to say that social work is *the art of adjusting personal relationships*, of helping to overcome the difficulties which may arise, for example, between employers and employees, between school and home.    These are just the things that each of us tries to do for himself and that we frequently try to do for our friends and neighbors. Most of us have not made a special study of such problems, of their causes, or of the scientific basis for their solution.    There would be much less confusion if the term social worker were reserved for people who have made such special studies and are trained in scientific methods of dealing with difficult problems of human relationships."

*Case Examples*.    Other effective ways of defining the field of social work may be found in concrete illustrations of various types, such as case records of individuals, of families, of communities, of social legislation, of social research, and many others.    Such illustrations will be found in the volumes upon which the study course in this book is based.    An excellent method of attempting to define the several aspects of social work would be for the student to state a problem and illustrate with a case under each of the several divisions approached. In social work, as in law, the case method of instruction is one of the most important methods of approach. The number of available books and other source material in this field is increasing rapidly. Such examples as *Three Problem Children*, *Children Astray*, and many other studies of examples of maladjusted boys, girls, and older folk, together with such teaching books as Breckinridge's *Family Welfare in a Metropolitan Community* will prove most effective not only to the professional social worker, but to the lay citizen as well.

*The Master Social Worker.* Another method of approaching the concept of social work might be found in the examples of outstanding leaders in the field of social work. For the purpose of this chapter two types of examples might be cited, the one the idealistic and historical Master Teacher, and the other concrete examples of the modern day. In many ways the Master Teacher might illustrate the Master Social Worker. He not only went about doing good, but His goodness invariably found its objectives in the bettering of human fortunes, the strengthening of human relations, the pointing of human destiny. A single illustration of the method and scope which His efforts exemplified will be found in the cases of healing and social adjustment recorded. Of the thirty-six cases with which I have recently renewed a hurried acquaintance, no less than thirty-two were of the essence and spirit of social work. As I interpret them each was performed as a result of an actual need which expressed itself in concrete form and social relationship. The need was before Him; the call of the individual, of humanity, could not be resisted, and so He performed the service. Healing the sick, but with the emphasis upon the personal effort of the client himself, and upon the social relationship of the deed and the need; alleviating suffering in body and spirit; centering a great love and social effort upon the defective, the delinquent, and the dependent, the Master Social Worker not only sought to bring men to normal power and life but He actually did it. Nor blind nor deaf, nor lame nor leper, nor broken hearted failed to find in Him a social physician. There was to Him no limitation of wealth or poverty, of clean or unclean, of happy or bereaved. The centurian or nobleman or widow—all alike were to Him great human cases calling for human adjustment. If sometimes He seemed to favor the poor, He never discriminated against the well-to-do or rich. One would search in vain to find a difference in method or spirit in His treatment of the widow's son, or the nobleman's first born. Always He saw the need; always He worked on this basis. Never could He let the needs go unmet. Never was there maudlin sentiment, but serious business and great compassion. Never was there superficial and egotistic self-advertisement; whenever opportunity came for this and the demand for display appeared, He was always disappointing to the crowds. But always He saw the crying need of the maladjusted individual who came in the way of His daily life. There was always method, but never the sacrifice of the individual for technique. There was always theory and good theory, of cause and effect, and there was remarkable wisdom and an unerring common sense in His adjustment of the problems of the individual and the group. Sometimes there was the community need, like the feeding of the multitudes, or the social occasion of the wedding. And always there was the great contribution which He made to the essence of community—the challenge to work together and to love neighbor as self.

*A Southern Leader.* The story of modern social work is, in many ways, the story of outstanding leaders. An excellent field of neglected biography might be found in the "case studies" of noble social workers of national leadership. One excellent project would be to review the story of the presidents of the fifty-three annual meetings of the National Conference of Social Work, and through them to trace the development and growth of a half century of social work. This however, is a larger task and is suggested here only as a type of approach to the whole field of social work. It will not be amiss, however, to quote here as a concrete illustration the resolution of The American Association for Organizing Family Social Work passed at the recent Cleveland Conference in memory of Joseph C. Logan, the pioneer social worker of the South.

He has become part of our history, we have become his heirs, and that is a heavy obligation. We have seen the blossoming of family case work and of social work in the South, the South awakening from the lethargy of the economic results of the Civil War and its heritage of prejudices, and yet keenly and finely comprehensive of the newly recognized social values in terms of human life and achievement. Joe Logan was *the* pioneer in the south, a great soul that was never damaged by the philosophy of content, of assuming that things could not be better "considering," of satisfaction with non-increasing progress. The first days of our field service were given to the South. Without Joe Logan's services the way would never have been opened, and indeed he was scarcely to be considered as other than a member of our staff. He is "Emeritus" now; but a splendid task, splendidly done, is his achievement. By reason of it, social work in the South has always had the greater glamour for those whose lives must be lived with high hopes and high efforts in accomplishing the impossible. Simple, fine, best of companions and friends, more ready to laugh at himself than others, but always ready to pluck the humor out of life, a well of enthusiasm and buoyancy which made the hardest task appear the easiest: We salute you, a dauntless and laughing cavalier. We salute a generous and gentle heart.

*Two Trends.* There are certain important trends in social work which indicate further the growth, development, and scope of its activities. There is, on the one hand, a continuing tendency to develop the specialist and the technician within the sub-divisions of the whole field of social work. There is, on the other hand, a growing consensus of opinion that many of the strongest social workers of the future will be general leaders of community and society, trained in the technique of social leadership and the development of personality. Both of these trends are important. Both may be developed into effective tools for the promotion of social work and public welfare, but it is important that each tendency be guided in accordance with special needs and fields. We may illustrate the specialization of training by reference to the technicians in family case work, child welfare, hospital social service, psychiatric social work, and other type specialization. Less specialized divisions of social work, but nevertheless requiring special types of training, are found in industrial welfare work, in rural social work, in urban community organization, and in public welfare. Illustrations of the field of work for the social leader with broad training in social science and well developed personality will be found in problems of rural social work, the county unit of public welfare, the field of public health education, and in college and university demands for teachers of social science who know how to make their work dynamic.

*A Specialized Type.* As an example of increasing specialization, the recently formed American Association of Psychiatric Social Workers may be cited. This newly formed organization grew naturally out of the original combination of Hospital Social Workers and Psychiatric Social Workers. Because of the growing field in each of these specialisms and the wide divergences of their methods and contacts, "the Section on Psychiatric Social Work of the American Association of Hospital Social Workers formally disbanded at its fourth annual meeting held at Cleveland on May 26, 1926, and a new independent organization, the American Association of Psychiatric Social Workers was formed. For the past year the members of the Section on Psychiatric Social Work have been considering, whether—in view of the relation of psychiatric social work to the whole field of social work—it would be to the best interests of the professional group of psychiatric social workers to continue as a part of a larger group whose interests are primarily medical, and centered to a large extent in hospitals. As the greatest developments in recent years in psychiatric social work have been outside of the hospital field and more closely allied to general social work, after careful consideration, the Section on Psychiatric Social Work decided to withdraw from the parent organization. The American Association of Hospital Social Workers has maintained cor-

dial relations with its Section during the past year
of indecision and has helped in every way to
facilitate the plans for reorganization.  The new
Association of Psychiatric Social Workers realizes
that it has been of inestimable value during the
period of initial growth to have been affiliated
with the larger, well-established professional group
of hospital social workers, and does not expect that
the separation will lessen the coöperation between
the two bodies."  The officials of The American
Association of Psychiatric Social Workers include
representatives of Boston Psychopathic Hospital,
Iowa Psychopathic Hospital, National Committee
for Mental Hygiene, Bureau of Children's Guidance, Michael Reese Dispensary, Illinois Society
for Mental Hygiene, Commonwealth Fund.  This
list of institutions is itself typical of the field of
psychiatric social work.

*Industrial Social Work.*  A less specialized type
of social work, but nevertheless requiring specialized training together with general leadership, is
that of industrial social work, variously called
welfare work, industrial betterment, community
service, and other terms.  It has been defined by
the Bureau of Labor Statistics as "anything for
the comfort and improvement, intellectual or

social, of the employees for and above wages paid,
which is not a necessity of the industry or required
by law." This whole field, lately developed into
a many-sided work, closely bound up with working conditions and leisure time activities, has a
most interesting history. From the mediaeval,
manorial customs through the later guilds' efforts
and agencies up through the Industrial Revolu-
tion to Robert Owen there has been an interesting
development. Similar developments may be
found in France, Germany, followed by New
England. The late nineteenth and twentieth
centuries saw a great increase in the number of
companies developing welfare work and a great
variety in their methods and scope. The whole
work developed rapidly until in 1926 Mr.
Abraham Epstein reported information on 1500
employers in the United States alone doing some
sort of social work in the midst of an estimated
4,000,000 workers. Like most phases of social
work, it began without the trained worker, with
very elementary and group efforts, and has advanced until it is in need of the ablest social
workers available. The whole story of industrial
social work in New England and the South will
make a volume of no mean proportions. In

North Carolina alone, there have been no less than 250 individual efforts towards some sort of industrial social work, while as many more might be found in the rest of the industrial South. All students of social work and public welfare will follow with great interest the effective development of this field of social work.    .

*Rural Social Work.*  Again, in the field of rural social work will be found another important illustration of some of the needs and developments in the whole field.  An experience both pathetic and humorous has been recorded in the story of the attempts of social workers to transplant the whole of urban methods and technique upon the soil of the open spaces.  So far as a clear record goes there has been no successful social work on a large scale. Here, then, is one of the larger tasks of the immediate future.  Professor Steiner has stated the problem well, as may be seen from the following quotation from his recent article, in *Social Forces*, on "The Basis of Procedure in Rural Social Work."

Lack of uniformity in rural conditions makes generalizations concerning rural social work very unsatisfactory. The customary division between rural and urban is helpful, but may become misleading by creating the impression that these two contrasting types of social situations are characterized by a large degree of uniformity wherever found. Social research in cities has long presented such convincing evidence of the wide divergencies between different types of cities as well as within the cities themselves, that urban social agencies accept as a matter of course the necessity for extensive variations in procedure so as to meet the needs of different groups and situations. Investigations of rural communities have also gone far enough to make clear the extraordinary contrasts in rural life that grow out of economic, topographical, and geographical conditions, but rural social work unfortunately has not yet sufficiently advanced to attempt seriously the necessary adjustments. For the most part we are still expending our energy in showing why urban social work technique cannot be transplanted bodily into rural areas, whereas what is really needed is a clear recognition that the vast differences in rural conditions may require various methods of approach in dealing with rural social problems. When one calls to mind the prosperous rural communities located in river valleys or on fertile plains; the scattered and run down farms in the rough, hilly sections where the soil has lost its fertility and transportation is difficult; the sparsely settled areas in some southern states characterized by one mule farms of low productivity or large plantations run by a poorly housed and inefficient tenant population; the agricultural areas adjacent to great cities where intensive truck farming and convenient access to city life produce problems peculiar to such situations; the great farm areas of the western plains where extensive farming and stock raising

have developed communities typical of that region, the
constantly expanding rural sections devoted to small
fruits and vegetables with their seasonal and child labor
problems; when one calls to mind these outstanding types
of rural areas which may still further be subdivided and
differentiated according to their degree of isolation,
density of population, quality of people, methods of
production, status of social institutions and of means
of transportation, it is quite obvious that rural social
work must be characterized by an exceedingly flexible
organization and technique that may only in its more
general features approximate a common type.   In certain
rural areas a rational development of social work may
lead in the direction of more effective alliances with
urban social agencies while in other places there may be
indicated a program of work designed specifically to deal
with the problems of a sparsely settled and isolated
rural population.   In any event rural social work must
not be thought of as a new technique of a distinctive type
but rather as extensive modifications of social work procedure to meet varying rural conditions."

*Steiner's Suggestions.*  Professor Steiner pro-
ceeds then to emphasize the importance of adequate study of rural areas, of sympathetic understanding of conditions, of scientific rather than
imaginary approach, of the need for genuine
experiment well grounded, and of the importance
of correlating with the economic situation, and of

the whole study of organization and background of rural situation. He recognizes, of course, the difficulties in the way and the necessity for time and patience. He says, "The fundamental difficulty is that there has been a widespread failure to understand just what is involved in the extension of social work to rural communities. The large mileage to be covered, the bad condition of the less frequented roads, the heavy expense of maintaining cars for field workers, the indifference of the people, and the lack of well equipped co-operating agencies, are a few of the many problems that must be faced by an agency that desires to carry on its work in the open country. Too often these difficulties loom up so large that the rural social work undertaken is only of a fragmentary sort that makes no pretense of covering the entire field. The fact is that the extension of social work in a thoroughgoing manner to the more isolated districts would require a much larger staff of skilled workers than could ordinarily be financed even by a joint rural-urban agency."

*Public Welfare Again.* Requiring specialized training and technique, alongside the mastery of general fundamentals of social work, is the field of public welfare as previously defined in this

chapter.   For the ordinary state program of public welfare there are several fundamental principles
involved.   In the first place, emphasis upon rural
social work and county organization is predomi-
nant.   Again the problem of community organization in the small town and village as well as the
problem of coöperation between county and city
will be of supreme importance.   Thus the same
essentials for future study, development, and work
as applied to the procedure in rural social work will
apply in general to the field of public welfare.
So, too, the more difficult problem of community
organization will be found in the attempt to
develop successful organization and administration of public welfare.   The second outstanding
characteristic of public welfare is the important
factor of governmental financing, control, and participation.   While voluntary and private social
work is essentially the citizen's business as a
member of the community, public welfare is the
citizen's business in the technical sense of his being
a member of the great corporation of government,
of which he is also a stockholder.   It touches him
in his general finances, in his taxes, in the degree in
which he wishes to develop a democratic government serving all the people.   It, therefore, be-

comes a problem of politics, both in the sense in which Aristotle called politics the noblest of all the sciences, and also unfortunately in the worse implications of political practice. Public welfare as social work thus brings into play many of the conflicting ideals and traditions of freedom, of interference with private affairs, of the old ideals of charity, and of the right of the many to be taxed by the few. It thus involves an educational problem of interpreting its meaning to the people. It involves larger techniques of economy and efficiency in business government and especially the problem of interpreting its importance to public officials and political leaders. One of its most difficult problems is that of coördinating public and private effort towards improving human welfare in all matters of social deficiency. How much private and philanthropic effort, how much governmental aid, what difficulties are there in this adjustment of private and public relationships? Public welfare is, therefore, a very integral part of the whole problem which political science faces to evolve a form of democratic government which will really give equal opportunity for all to develop normal life and happiness. The fact that the problem is a difficult one offers the more attractive challenge for the able student or practitioner in social work to attempt more effective results. That much success is being accomplished is everywhere in evidence. In every state in the union there are increasingly earnest and effective efforts to study the problem and to establish economic and scientific systems of public welfare. In more than thirty of the states there are definite organizations worthy of emulation. Two later chapters in this volume will be devoted to the State and City as problem studies in public welfare and social work.

*The Broader Leadership.* An examination, therefore, of the unusual demands upon social work and the social worker in the fields of industrial, rural, and public welfare social work will indicate something of the importance of fundamental training in social leadership and of the development of well selected personalities. That is, it is necessary first of all to provide leaders whose background is based upon adequate knowledge and generous experience, whose social practice is based upon a broad sympathy and deep understanding of the problems involved, and whose personalities are such as to direct the people and work into harmonious paths. There is, therefore, developing an important trend in the education and training of social workers to supplement and parallel the specialization which has been developed, as already indicated. Thus the social worker must be prepared to make his contacts and perform his services over a relatively large area and in a relatively varying number of fields. He will select his assistants with this general policy in view. Both he and his assistants may need to cover several phases of the work within a given area rather than to perform a single technique over the entire jurisdiction. The public health nurse may need also to be a case worker and to know how to coöperate in matters of nutrition, home economics, and child welfare. The superintendent of public welfare must needs know the field of the visiting teacher, he must know much of community history and organization, he must know something of family case work, he must keep abreast of the modern advances in juvenile delinquency, crime and punishment, poverty and dependency. And he must know something of office administration and organization. This, it must be admitted, is an unusual requirement for a social worker or any other leader. It must be admitted, on the other hand, that there is no task

more important and that there must be no undue
haste in the training of such workers and in the
plans for developing effective social leadership.
This tendency to train general leaders rather than
the special technician in no wise detracts from the
importance of specialization or the demand for
leaders trained intensively within the special field
of social work.   It is rather a challenge to see that
both types of leadership are developed.   It is a
challenge for the training of men as social workers
as well as women.   It is a challenge for social
work to take its place rightfully alongside of the
other professions of education, law, medicine,
ministry.   It is a challenge to coördinate social
work with institutional development.

*The Social Sciences*.   It will be seen, therefore,
that one of the most important tasks of social
work is that of utilizing the social sciences in the
study and working out of its social problems in
much the same way as the physical sciences have
been utilized to develop good roads, factories,
and the other varied phases of material development.   Just as the great advances made in
physics, chemistry, engineering, and other physical
sciences have contributed to the marvelous development of economic and material welfare,

so economics, sociology, history, government, anthropology, social psychology, statistics, jurisprudence, and the other social sciences must be utilized in the scientific adjustment of social relationships. Just as the loyal and devoted efforts of the physical scientists, working faithfully over long periods of time have been rewarded by great success, so the zeal and persistency of the social scientists must ultimately bring to bear upon social work great contributions of value. Social study, social research, social work—all must go hand in hand in the new era of the development of human relationships.

*Training for Social Work.* A final measure of the scope and progress of social work may be found in the constantly enlarging plans and systems for the training of social workers. In the American Association of Schools of Professional Social Work alone, covering the United States and Canada, there are no less than twenty-four institutions which provide courses or schools of training for social workers. In addition to these, Miss Sydnor Walker, of the Laura Spelman Rockefeller Memorial, in her study of training for social work has given some data on still another score of schools which claim to offer some sort of training for the social worker. Dr. René Sands lists more than three score schools of social study in foreign countries including Great Britain, Belgium, Chile, Czechoslovakia, Finland, France, Germany, Italy, Netherlands, South Africa, Sweden, and Switzerland. These vary greatly, of course, but indicate something of the *science* of the movement for training social workers.

*The American Association.* The list of American schools is indicative of the geographical and educational range of the present effort. The Association of Schools of Professional Social Work include the following:

> Bryn Mawr College
> National Catholic Service School
> Indiana University
> Loyola University
> McGill University
> University of Michigan
> University of Chicago
> Carnegie Institute
> Johns Hopkins University
> University of Missouri
> University of Minnesota
> New York School of Social Work
> University of North Carolina
> Ohio State University

University of Oregon
Western Reserve University
University of Wisconsin
University of Southern California
University of Toronto
Pennsylvania School of Social Work and Public
    Health
Simmons College
Smith College

*Principles.* The general requirements and principles underlying the training of social workers as outlined by a committee of the association will give another important means of interpreting the needs and principles of social work. The following requirements have been stated:

In view of the diversity of courses of instruction for training social workers and the variety of administrative systems under which the instruction is given—systems which include separate schools, graduate and undergraduate schools or departments of endowed colleges and universities and of state universities, as well as schools under the auspices of religious denominations, and the apprentice and institute courses of national service organization—the Executive Committee of the Association of Training Schools for Professional Social Work considers it desirable to make at this time a statement of the fundamental principles underlying adequate professional education for social work. The Committee hopes that this statement may be a service to those who contemplate the establishment of new schools, as well as to those concerned with the determination of policies for the existing schools.

1. Data collected from social workers and special investigations that have been made recently show clearly that the most satisfactory preparation for social work is that which is conducted on a broad basis of professional education. Preparation of this character utilizes the technical contributions of allied professions, requires unity and continuity of instruction, and is contingent upon centralized responsibility of direction and administration.

2. It is highly desirable, in order to meet these requirements, that a school offering preparation for social work should approximate the following specific organization, whether as an educational unit it be separate from, affiliated with, or constitute a part of a larger educational institution:

A. An organic grouping of relevant courses of instruction into a special curriculum for the stated purpose of vocational training or professional education for social work.

B. These grouped courses of instruction should consist, in general, of four types:

(1) *Background or pre-professional courses*, to be given by a regular member or members of the faculty in good academic standing.

(2) *Specific knowledge courses*, providing a broad scientific equipment for social work, to be given by specialists in good professional standing outside the field of social work.

     (3) *Technical knowledge courses*, dealing with special branches of social work, together with clinical field work, to be given by one or more social workers eligible for senior membership in the American Association of Social Workers, with adequate academic qualifications for teaching, whose further status is that of salaried and voting members of the faculty of the school.

     (4) *Technical training courses*, to provide the skill which a practitioner must possess, consisting chiefly of intensive field work centrally supervised and directed by one or more social workers eligible to senior membership in the American Association of Social Workers, with adequate academic qualifications for teaching, whose further status is that of salaried (at least half-time) and voting members of the faculty of the school.

  C. An administrator or director chosen or appointed as the executive head of the school, who is empowered, in coöperation with the faculty of the school, to exercise control over admission requirements, curriculum, credit basis for class-room and field work, and admission requirements to courses of instruction.

3. Professional education for medical social service, psychiatric social work, probation work, visiting teaching, and other specialized forms of social case work, requires the coöperation of allied professions and the utilization of the resources of hospital, dispensary, court, school, and

other social agencies. Careful planning and close supervision is necessary to make these working relationships
effective educationally. Without pre-professional requirements, unity and correlation in the curriculum, and centralized administrative responsibility, it is impossible to
provide adequately for the training of the prospective
social worker.

*Added Evidence for Public Welfare.* A new
book just published in July, 1926, by the W. B.
Saunders Company is entitled *Social Work A
Family Builder*, by Harriet Townsend, lecturer
in social science at Teachers College, Columbia
University. This little volume is of particular
interest in this discussion because it is prepared,
not primarily for the professional social worker,
but for the public health nurses, dietitians, home
demonstration agents, and special teachers. That
is, it aims to interpret social work to those specialists in the field of public health, public education
and other fields of public service. In the fourteen chapters are important discussions of reasons
for social work, the background for social work,
contrast between the old and new practice, problems of the American and immigrant families in a
changing world, the family standard of living, the
scientific approach to the problem, diagnosis and

treatment of a family problem, and a general discussion of the relation of public and private agencies. Miss Townsend agrees with the thesis of this little volume that there is more and more need for governmental participation in social work. Special emphasis is put upon the importance of the scientific basis for public social service with the emphasis upon the extension of the area of social justice. The last chapter in this volume is an excellent discussion of the relation of public welfare to social work. In a previous chapter Miss Townsend says: "With the conclusion of this case, which on the whole was satisfactorily handled, the mind naturally questions the organization of society which leaves the financial burden and social treatment of this important disease to a private relief agency."

*A Growing Literature.* Many other new books appearing and soon to appear afford new evidence of the increasing definiteness and accuracy of social work and public welfare development. In addition to the new volume just mentioned there are two or three volumes now in preparation dealing with the scope and field of social work. Dr. Robert W. Kelso, formerly Commissioner of Public Welfare in Massachusetts and now executive of the Boston Council of Social Agencies, has nearly completed a volume on *The Science of Public Welfare*, which will be published shortly in the Henry Holt American Social Science Series. Dr. Kelso's book was prepared with special reference to the difficulties and problems suggested in this volume.   Two volumes dealing with the training of social workers have appeared, while many articles have been contributed to the current periodicals.   In the next chapter reference will be made to the volumes on education and training for social work, by Professors Steiner and Tufts, while the primary basis of study in the third chapter will be that of *The Equipment of the Social Worker*, by Elizabeth Macadam.   Other volumes of special interest include Halbert's *What is Professional Social Work?*  Queen's *Social Work in the Light of History*, Mary Richmond's *What is Social Case Work?* and *Social Diagnosis*, and the two important little volumes just published by the American Association of Social Workers under the titles of *The Nature and Scope of Social Work* and *Vocational Aspects of Family Social Work*.  Besides these and other books, many valuable current articles may be found in *The Survey, The Family, Social Forces, Opportunity*, and other journals of social study and social work.

# CHAPTER II

## THE EQUIPMENT OF THE SOCIAL WORKER

*The Social Worker a First Essential.* A review
of the previous chapter naturally leaves the impression that the most important task in the whole
field of public welfare and social work is the problem of equipping the student, the social scientist,
and the social worker for their tasks. A brief
review of the requirements of the social worker
and of the opportunity for his training will not
only point out important tasks to be done by the
individual and by associations for the development of social work, but will in a large measure
help to review the fundamentals of social work and
give important applications to public welfare and
social direction, in different form from that in the
previous chapter. Chapter II, therefore, will
consist of a simple study-outline with questions
based upon the book, *The Equipment of the Social
Worker*, by Elizabeth Macadam, and published
by Henry Holt and Company, in 1925. Supplementary readings will be based on *Education and
Training for Social Work*, by Professor James H.
Tufts of the University of Chicago, published by

the Russell Sage Foundation; and *Education for Social Work*, by Professor Jesse F. Steiner of the University of North Carolina, published by the University of Chicago Press.

*The Newer Emphasis Upon Social Work.* Social work, like other professions and new movements, has necessarily developed slowly. Like public education and public health, it has been misunderstood and misinterpreted. Like other movements, it has made its mistakes and has had its limitations. It is even now but beginning to assume form and content adequate to attract the attention of the public and to warrant due confidence. Some of the phases of social work have been discussed in Chapter I. It is very clear, however, that the first essential for successful social work must be found in the well equipped social worker. Again and again social work has failed temporarily because of the lack of personality, common sense, and training of the worker upon whom difficult tasks have fallen. This need not be considered a matter for discouragement in any way or in any sense. It is rather a matter of time and training. The whole problem of training for social work involves a beginning in the study of social problems and an understanding of the modern social emphasis and trend. It involves the gradual training of workers in the field and of recruiting new workers as rapidly as needed.

1. Why is the modern movement for social study and social work attracting so little attention?
2. According to Macadam, what is meant by social work?
3. Distinguish between social work and social study.

*History of Social Work Training.* In studying the historical development of training for social work, one is impressed with a similarity to the development of public education. In the matter of certification of teachers and of standards there has been a long trail from small beginnings over rough ways to the present highways of modern teacher training. There is a similar resemblance to the administration of school affairs. In the old days county superintendents of schools were often part-time men with little opportunity and resources. Now they have been given status adequate for real work, and yet in the development of public education, through all of its difficulties, there was no tendency to accuse the whole public education system of inefficiency or to demolish its organization. The same attitude ought to be taken towards social work and public welfare.

4. Trace the beginnings of social training from 1890–1903.
5. Outline briefly the development of social training from 1903–1926.
6. What are the three aims of social work as found in the first thirty years' experiment?

*University Training.* Within recent years there has been a considerable movement toward the introduction of courses for social workers in the college or university curricula. In Chapter I the list of American universities with training schools or formal courses was given. This development of education for social work has increased with the newer movements to make colleges and universities adequate for the needs of the modern era. It also represents, however, a different emphasis upon training. The old plan was that of apprenticeship, while the new is that of technical training combined with field work. Needless to say, there are advantages and disadvantages in both systems. The problem is to utilize both plans to the best advantage, always keeping in mind the selection and development of good personalities, and combining adequate technical training with common sense leadership.

7. Why is the university rather than outside centers the best basis for scientific social study?
8. What are some of the limitations of the university?
9. Discuss the opportunity for academic study.
10. What are the requirements of university certificates in social work?
11. Discuss the "field" or practical work opportunities of the universities.
12. Discuss the difficulties and limitations of field work in the university.
13. Give a concrete illustration of field work directed by a university.

*Specialized Fields of Training.* In Chapter I types of special social work were discussed. For such work, of course, there must be special, or specially trained workers. For the social worker there must be adequate background in the social sciences, and in each speciality there must be particular emphasis upon particular subjects. Economics and economic backgrounds are of especial importance in industrial social work; psychology in psychiatric social work; government and community organization in public welfare social work, and so on for the others.

14. What special requirements are needed for training in factories and workshops?
15. What is the relation of industrial psychology to social work?
16. What is meant by hospital social service?
17. What is meant by social work in the public services?
18. Contrast the British public service with American public welfare.
19. Give an outline of a considerable training course in college or university.

*Social Work and Institutions.* One interpretation of social work, given by Professor Tufts, referred to its relation to the institutions. As a matter of fact, social work must operate through institutions and social organizations. We have sometimes referred to the institutions, such as the family, the school, and the state as being buffers to go between the individual and social and economic change. Thus the institutions become both a chief mode and a means through which the social worker must perform his tasks.

20. Discuss the church in relation to social work.

21. Discuss medicine in relation to social work.
22. Discuss education in relation to social work.
23. Discuss law in relation to social work.
24. Discuss the citizen in relation to social work.

*The Future of Social Work.* A study of fifty years of progress, as measured by the National Conference of Social Work, reveals not only an interesting past but a promising future for social work. But it also indicates, if we are to judge by the past, that the future will be much different from the present. Social workers should be warned, therefore, not to be dogmatic on the one hand or impatient on the other. They will realize that in this field more than any other "A little learning is a dangerous thing," but that much learning can be gained gradually by steady effort and a measure of humility, alongside the scientific attitude of mind.

25. Give concrete examples of training schools for social work in America.
26. Contrast American training with that in other countries.
27. Discuss the general future of social work.
28. What are the special needs and limitations of social work in the South?

*Steiner on Education for Social Work.* The first volume to be published on education for social work was that written by Professor Steiner, in 1920. Professor Steiner points out that the term social work was not used at the opening of the present century, but that such terms as philanthropy, charity, correction, outdoor relief, and the like were most commonly employed. He calls attention to the fact that the first appeal for professional training was sought under the auspices of "A Training School in Applied Philanthropy." The following questions are based upon Professor Steiner's little volume:

29. Discuss the contrast between the old methods of cure and the present methods of prevention in social work.
30. Discuss the apprenticeship method of training social workers in the United States.
31. Discuss the relation of sociology to social work in the past.
32. What general education is required for admission to schools of social work in the United States?
33. What is the case method of instruction?
34. What is meant by the social work laboratory?
35. What is a social work clinic?

*Tufts on Education and Training for Social Work.*    A second volume on *Education and Training for Social Work* was published by the Russell Sage Foundation in 1922, and embodied a comprehensive report made by Professor James H. Tufts of the University of Chicago.   In his 235 pages, he has reviewed many of the older phases of social work, but has also added many others. We have already quoted his definition of social work in terms of fields.

36. What does he mean by border fields which concern the family or government or recreation?
37. What does he mean by asking if social work is a woman's profession?
38. What are some of the prejudices against social work?
39. Should training for social work be graduate or undergraduate?
40. How does the range of salaries of social workers compare with that of other professions?

SPECIAL QUESTIONS FOR STUDY AND
ILLUSTRATION

I. *Commonsense Equipment.*    Woodrow Wilson has been cited often as an example of the man

to whom a typewriter was a constant companion and a good friend. To the social
worker this citation needs no new emphasis.
Day in and day out he must needs know how,
and be willing to work out plans and outlines.
Thus social workers are urged to learn to use
this tool. Another requirement of the School
of Public Welfare at the University of North
Carolina is that of driving a Ford or other
car. Here again will be found the indispens-
able companion of the social worker.

What other commonsense equipment
should be listed?

II. *Material Equipment.* The use of a typewriter and Ford do not in any sense imply a
neglect of due assistance in office and in field.
In order to do his work well the social worker
needs ample help in office, in filing and keeping records, and in specialized social work in
the field. One of the surest ways to realize
on an investment in public welfare is to give
the superintendent a good chance to work
well.

What are the requirements of a good
office?

III. *Winning the Folks.* A young woman went
into a rural and mountain county where
social work was unknown and not understood. She helped a farmer plow one day in
an emergency. She taught as substitute for

sick teachers. She helped a county official straighten out his books and balance his accounts. She helped the solicitor with his cases in court. She kept moderately good case records.

To what extent was she justified in neglecting record keeping for community work of this sort?

IV. *Coöperating with the Churches.* A superintendent of public welfare regularly enlists the help of his churches in town and country. Some of the ministers feel that such work is important, others think not so much of it. What is more important than their work in prison camps and county home, unless it be their combined efforts to keep folks from becoming inmates of these institutions? A minister in another county thought that it was not worth while to go to the chain gangs because most of the folks were negroes.

Criticise this attitude.

V. *Personality and Morale.* The late President G. Stanley Hall brings out a new emphasis in his book on *Morale* when he defines morale as "the cult of condition." For the social worker nothing is more important than keeping in condition. At the last National Conference at Cleveland Mr. Porter Lee of the New York School emphasized in a vigorous way the importance of personality.

We have an idea that personality and morale are closely connected—illustrate how.

VI. *The Worth of Directing Human Affairs.* If physicians, lawyers, ministers, teachers, business officials, must needs have training and certificates of proficiency for their work of directing special phases of human activities, how much more important for those who direct human destinies to aspire to broad training and effective work? Shaw used to say something about "those who can do, those who can't teach."

Is this the danger in social work also?

# CHAPTER III

## GENERAL MODERN SOCIAL PROBLEMS AND TRENDS

*The Importance of Social Study.* It has been pointed out that one of the most important tasks of the present era is the scientific study of modern social problems, and that methods should be employed as scientific as those in the study and development of industrial, economic, and engineering problems. A good approach to the study of modern social problems and social trends will be found in *Problems of Citizenship*, by Baker-Crothers and Hudnut, published in 1925 by Henry Holt and Company. Not all of the major social problems are discussed in this volume, but the authors have attempted in both method and content an approach to a sufficient number of social problems to make an admirable beginning. Their first approach is a discussion of America's ideals of freedom and independence. Recent developments make it clear that they have been justified in considering this as an American problem. The questions in this chapter are all based directly upon the text.

*The Newspaper Problem.* (Chapters 2, 3.) The newspaper as a social force and as a medium of carrying to the people not only news but information concerning public policy is each year becoming more and more important. The newspaper can be used both to study social problems and to promote social work:

41. What are the three general things to be remembered in intelligent newspaper reading? Explain.
42. What is meant by press service? Name chief ones.

*The Immigration Problem.* (Chapters 4, 5, 6, 7.) The problems of immigration are of vital importance in all studies of population and national development. In the United States the problem has been accentuated since the war and new laws have been passed. The problem is of importance in the whole newer trends toward international coöperations. It is important in the South especially because of the general attitude of the South towards immigration and because of the recent migration of negroes North and West. On the western coast the Japanese situation is of great importance.

43. Name and differentiate the four attitudes toward immigration.
44. What are the important provisions of the immigration laws of 1917, of 1921 and 1922, and 1924?
45. Where do the majority of immigrants settle? What is the effect on native industrial worker of influx of large number of immigrants?
46. Give date and explain Gentleman's Agreement between United States and Japan.
47. What is Land Law of 1913? the Act of 1920?
48. What provision of the immigration law of 1924 affects the Japanese? Explain.

*The Negro Problem.* (Chapters 8, 9, 10, 11.) The negro problem, which has been considered a Southern problem only, has become a concern of nation-wide importance. The migration of more than a million negroes north, and their concentration in a relatively small number of communities has brought the problem face to face with other sections of the country. The negro problem, however, is still of utmost importance in the South and needs more careful study and more sympathetic attention than it has ever had. Some natural questions are:

Has the recent migration of negroes been good or bad for the negro, good or bad for the white man, good or bad for the South, good or bad for the North, good or bad for the nation.  Other questions are:

49. Give chief provisions of 14th and 15th Amendments.   How evaded by the states?
50. Why is it urgent to improve educational facilities for the negro?
51. Discuss the negro in agriculture, as an industrial worker.
52. What were the causes of the negro migration during the World War?
53. What were the essential points of President Harding's Birmingham address?
54. Give briefly the views of the conservative school in regard to negro development,— of the liberal group led by Dr. Du Bois.
55. What are the aims of the inter-racial commission?

*The Woman Problem.*   (Chapters 12, 13, 14, 15, 16.)   The least important of the problems of the readjustment of life and labor between men and women is the technical one of voting as expressed in the 19th Amendment.   There are other very important problems involved, women in industry, in politics, in general civic life in relation to the family and in relation to the general culture and professional life of society. The history of the woman movement is one of the most interesting of all the studies of social concern:

56. Explain mother right, patriarchy.
57. What is Declaration of Sentiments?
58. When was the 19th Amendment first introduced into Congress and when finally passed?
59. What is the aim of the modern woman movement?
60. What is the difference between the League of Woman Voters and the National Woman's Party?
61. What are some of the inequalities still existing which women are seeking to have removed?
62. What are the arguments advanced for higher wages for men? Discuss.
63. Explain briefly the Classification Act of 1923.

*The Industrial Problem.* (Chapters 17, 18, 19, 20, 21, 22, 23.) Many students of the modern era consider the problem of the readjustment of life and labor as between employer and employee the most critical one. Some there are who conclude that great progress is being made in the whole field of democracy as it relates to industry. Others are uneasy lest modern society will not learn its lesson from past experiences. At best, the problem is a complicated one and ought to have the most careful study and coöperation of all leaders and of all of the social institutions.

64. Explain doctrine of laissez faire or individualism that has dominated the modern era of society.
65. Define trade union, industrial union, labor union.
66. What is the advantage of a union, what actual results have been gained by unions?
67. Explain each of the following as used in connection with the conflict between labor and capital—injunction, spy, scab, strikebreaker, blacklist, strike, lockout, picket, boycott, sabotage.
68. Define: open shop, closed shop, open union shop, preferential union shop.
69. What are some of the peaceful methods used by workers and employers to solve their problems?
70. What is the Rochester Agreement?
71. Give main features of the Kansas Industrial Court.
72. Give reasons for and against government ownership of railroads.

73. Explain the Rochdale Coöperation Movement. Name other fields which have been developed by coöperative enterprise.
74. Give difference between socialism and anarchism.
75. What is I. W. W.?

*Problems of Civil Liberty.* (Chapters 24, 27.) The recent celebration of the 100th anniversary of the death of Thomas Jefferson was felt by many students of modern conditions to be a renewal of the American spirit of tolerance and freedom. Likewise, in the sesquicentennial celebration at Philadelphia, there are many opportunities for studying the varying degrees of progress in American life during the 150 years since the birth of the nation. Here again the history of the movement for human freedom proves a fascinating one:

76. Why are the Magna Carta, Petition of Right and Bill of Rights important documents? Give date of each.
77. What are fundamental principles set forth in Declaration of Independence and Constitution of the United States?
78. What was the Espionage Act of 1917 and 1918?
79. Explain Lusk Laws—date of passage, purpose and outcome.

80. Discuss briefly expulsion of Socialists from New York Assembly.
81. Discuss prevention of freedom of speech and of the press by the government in time of war.

*The Problem of International Relations.* (Chapters 28, 29.) Among the six most important world-wide problems we have commonly listed the problems of the readjustment between nation and nation as one. Whatever else may be true the old policies of isolation can no longer be maintained by any modern nation. What substitutes to offer, what adjustments to make—these are important questions to be answered.

82. What are the three main policies that have dominated the relations of the United States with other nations?
83. Give date and three principles of Monroe Doctrine.
84. What is the American View of Pan-Americanism?
85. In general what has been the part of the United States in the various European conferences?
86. What are the American policies that apply particularly to Asia?
87. In what way does our policy in Asia differ from our attitude toward European affairs?

*The Problem of War and Peace.* (Chapters 30, 31.) The complaint has sometimes been made that one of the difficulties of democracy was that the democratic government could not wage war effectively. In earlier times this might have been a serious objection. If the newer ideals of peace shall come to pass this will be but an added asset to the whole philosophy of democracy. Undoubtedly, one of the most critical questions of the modern world is the eternal query as to how to prevent war and how to promote peace.

88. Name and explain three causes of war.
89. How has international arbitration promoted peace? How have conferences?
90. What is League of Nations? Give reasons for or against entrance of United States into the League.

*Social Realism in Literature.* One of the most effective and concrete ways of studying both specific and general social problems is through the reading of fiction, which is critically realistic. For the student of social problems and the social worker, *Teef Tallow* by Stribling, and *Barren Ground* by Ellen Glasgow, both published by Doubleday, Page, and Company, afford a realistic background for the study of Southern social deficiencies.   In the reading of such books, of course, the student must continuously keep his scientific attitude.   Other volumes of fiction dealing with other special problems may be found if the student and social worker wish to proceed further.

SPECIAL QUESTIONS FOR STUDY AND<br>ILLUSTRATION

VII. *Important Social Relationships*.   It has been suggested that the most important "general" social problem in our midst is that of getting along with each other in group fashion.   Professor Ross speaks of "social peace."   In his little volume, published by the University of North Carolina Press, entitled *Roads to Social Peace*, he points out remedies which will help the town man and the country man to get along and work together better; also the employer and employee as well as the different religious organizations and the different states and sections.

Illustrate examples where there have been misunderstandings between town and country.

VIII. *The Country Life Problem*.   In the next chapter emphasis is placed upon the human side of the farmer's work and ideals.   There are many who believe the country life problem is among the most important at the present time. In a state like North Carolina and other Southern states the question of making the farm pay, of helping work out recreation programs, and, in general, of making country life more attractive is an imminent one.

Are there communities in your county where the population is gradually moving into towns? Where people are poorer today than a decade ago?

IX. *Regional and Sectional Problems.* Are the attitudes of Southern folk toward the general social problems studied different from those of other sections? What peculiar problems belong to the South in matter of race, immigration, "100% Americanism," religion, and others? Professor Edwin Mims has recently written a volume, published by Doubleday, Page and Company, entitled *The Advancing South*, in which he points out certain types of progress.

Illustrate exact ways in which your county has advanced in the last decade.

X. *The Development of Leadership.* In a little book entitled *Southern Pioneers in Social Interpretation*, and published by the University of North Carolina Press, Howard W. Odum, the editor, has expressed the conclusion that the South has not had enough experience in the last fifty years in the best leadership, has not had universities, has not developed an atmosphere of freedom, and has not rewarded distinguished effort.

Are the present leaders in your county the children of the leaders of the last generation?

# CHAPTER IV

## PROBLEMS OF SOCIAL DEFICIENCY AND WASTE

*Complex Social Relationships.* In a complex society, such as modern civilization is developing with its artificial congestion in cities, its industrial era, its supermechanical trends, and its common mode of excitement and haste, it is but natural that many abnormal social problems arise. While there are many who overemphasize the abnormal problems of society, and still others overemphasize the abnormal aspects of the individual, it is true, nevertheless, that one of the largest blocks of social problems will be found in the whole field of social pathology. This is especially true from the viewpoint of the social worker who seeks both preventive and remedial measures. Social deficiencies include a wide range of pathological conditions, such as the dependents, delinquents, and defectives; and the newer deficiencies in the field of mental and social hygiene. One aim of public welfare is to see that every individual has the maximum opportunity for the maximum expression of normal life. To put it negatively, its purpose is to reduce abnormality to the minimum and normal development to the maximum.

The first essential, however, for the development of a normal society is an adequate understanding of its abnormal and pathological phases. To understand something of their manifestation and causes, as well as remedies, is a first task of great importance. The next study, therefore, will be a study of the general field of social pathology, the questions for which will be based upon Queen's *Social Pathology*, published in 1926 by Lippincott. A second brief study in mental and social hygiene will be based upon the little volume, *Three Problem Children*, published by the Committee on the Prevention of Delinquency.

*Family Disorganization and Personal Demoralization.* (Chapters 1, 2, 3, 4, 5, 6, 7, 8, 9, 10, 11.) Since the family is the basic, organic social institution through which the individual not only comes into society, but through which he begins his social training, it must be evident that family disorganization would always produce abnormal conditions and personal demoralization. The whole question of family disorganization, with its many ramifications and causes, in the modern day provides one of the most technical approaches to the whole field of social work. The number of factors involved are too numerous to cover in any one treatment, but the following questions will make a good beginning:

91. What are the various approaches to an understanding of any person or group? What use must be made of them?
92. Define crisis, unadjustment, maladjustment, demoralization, disorganization.
93. How are problems met of widow with small children? Discuss.
94. What are the important factors leading to divorce?
95. Explain Court of Domestic Relations.
96. Discuss education as a means of preventing divorce.
97. Give and explain classification of deserters.
98. What are the three stages of treatment in desertion cases?
99. What should be function of agency in regard to child after placement in a private home?
100. Describe an institution at its best.
101. Discuss Juvenile Court as a protective agency.
102. What items should be included in a program for the elimination of child neglect?
103. Give some of the chief factors in the causation of problem children.

104. Discuss the Visiting Teacher as an agent dealing with problem children.
105. Explain child guidance and habit clinics.
106. According to Kammerer's analysis, what are the three most frequent causative factors in illegitimacy?
107. What are the hazards of the illegitimate child?
108. What are four remedies suggested for the prevention of illegitimacy?
109. Name and explain the activities of agencies active in the field of prevention of prostitution.
110. Give classification of homeless men.
111. Give program of prevention suggested by the United States Commission on Industrial Relations, and the plan of the Chicago Council of Social Agencies.
112. How is status of old age influenced by family connections? economic and personal factors?
113. Discuss industrial pensions.
114. Give details of British pension system.

*Economic Aspects of Social Disorganization and Personal Demoralization.* (Chapters 12, 13, 14, 15, 16, 17, 18, 19.) Many students of social disorganization have felt that the economic problem was the chief one leading to family disintegration and personal demoralization, although such a conclusion is scarcely justified. There can be no doubt that the elements of poverty, of the standard of living, of the psychological factors involved, where the earning power is broken, and all other economic factors are primary causes of social disorganization. Some phases of this problem have been suggested in the previous study of industrial problems, and still others will be approached in the next chapter on the human factors in industry. The following questions are of importance in the approach to one particular phase of social disorganization:

115. Give definition of poverty, standard of living.
116. What is minimum budget for family of five according to Queen? What proportion of incomes reached that level?
117. Explain the two great factors to be considered in the study of poverty.
118. What are some of the consequences of being poor?
119. What are types of irregular employment?
120. Name industries in which employment is irregular.
121. What are the social, and personal results of irregular labor?

122. How does the unemployed man become the unemployable?
123. Discuss the Chicago Unemployment Agreement of 1923.
124. Discuss fully effects of employment of women—physical, personal, domestic.
125. What is effect of employment of mother on children?
126. Why has woman gained more through legislation than through the trade union?
127. Discuss fully physical consequences of child labor.
128. What is effect of child labor on education? future industrial life?
129. Give briefly history of federal child labor legislation.
130. What is fatigue? Give some of the industrial causes.
131. What is effect of short rest period on output?
132. What are chief causes of industrial accidents?
133. Did employer or employee benefit under the old common law provision covering industrial accident?
134. In general what is purpose of workmen's compensation acts?
135. Give classification of disasters.
136. What are the after effects of disasters?

*Health Aspects of Social Disorganization and Personal Demoralization.* (Chapters 20, 21, 22, 23, 24, 25, 26, 27.)  One of the most encouraging phenomena of the modern era is that of the remarkable progress made in medicine and health programs.  The whole field of public health and preventive medicine represent marvelous progress second only to that of the modern era of industrial, mechanical, and material invention.  The death rate has been reduced, the span of life increased, while almost unbelievable strides have been made in the prevention of suffering.  Nevertheless, this whole field has yet many problems to be worked out, and furnishes the cause of much social disorganization and personal demoralization.  In the questions which follow it must be remembered that the word health refers to mental and social health as well as to physical health.

137. What are the most common causes of physical failure?
138. Discuss the British system of health insurance.
139. From what sources has opposition to such a plan come in this country?
140. Discuss problems connected with the promotion of health.

141. What are the predisposing causes of tuberculosis? Explain.
142. Explain Atro Workshop as example of vocational readjustment of tubercular patients. Why necessary?
143. What is the importance economically and socially of heart disease?
144. What are the causes direct and indirect of heart disease?
145. What are consequences of physical disability?
146. What is treatment of disabled soldiers and sailors?
147. Give difference between organic and functional nervous diseases.
148. What is the purpose of the psychiatric clinic?
149. Explain the term idiot, imbecile, moron.
150. Discuss colony care for mental defectives.
151. What are the social consequences of alcoholism?
152. Give briefly a history of attempted control of opium traffic.

*Social Reorganization and the Remaking of Personality.* (Chapters 28, 29.) One of the most important of the modern trends in social thinking is the newer emphasis placed upon the social personality. The subject of individual differences and social differentiation has come into newer emphasis alongside of the old discussions of social likeness. The whole subject has been brought forcibly to the attention of students and social workers in many ways. One is through the recent emphasis and advance in the study of social pathology; another is through the new field of psychiatry; another is through the recent emphasis upon social hygiene. The intelligence tests for children and the army tests for adults have added their quota. Both the saner and scientific aspects of these studies and the extreme and unscientific phases have alike brought out the importance of giving more emphasis to the individual and the social personality. Here is an important development in the whole field of democracy and one which offers tremendous opportunity for blunder as well as for progress. The following questions merely approach the subject:

153. Discuss need for the modification and expansion of the educational system.
154. Discuss the use of leisure time.
155. Give possible results of a crisis.
156. In addition to the remaking of personality, what does the solution of the problems of social pathology require?

SPECIAL QUESTIONS FOR STUDY AND
ILLUSTRATION

XI. *Mental Hygiene.* Reference has been made
to the special field of psychiatric social
work. Perhaps there has been no field of
social interest and effort which has developed more new material and methods
than the treatment and study of the
mentally deficient. There is a growing
conviction, even in lay circles, that the
mentally sick are at least as important
as the physically sick. And what of their
effect on posterity? What of the relation
of mental abnormality to vice, crime, poverty, and the other social deficiencies?

Estimate the number and nature of the
mentally deficient in a community, or in
a county.

XII. *Social Hygiene.* Of the physically sick no
group has become so great a burden to
society as those afflicted with the "social"
diseases. In the whole realm of social
problems no situations have been more
difficult or baffling than those which have
arisen from sex maladjustments. Here
again social science has attempted to get at
the facts and great progress has been made.
Nevertheless there is no field in which the
social worker is inclined to be more awk-

ward or in which he needs to work more carefully or in which he needs more knowledge and skill.

Outline a simple social hygiene program for a rural county.

XIII. *Family Relationships.* In the spring of 1926 the University of North Carolina Senior Class requested that a series of lectures be given to them on the subject of family relationships. They wanted these lectures because they expected to found new families and they professed general ignorance. Thus it is brought to the attention of educators that colleges do not teach family relationships, although holding the family to be the most important institution. The course was given and included lectures on the family in modern life, the history of the family, commonsense sex adjustments, woman in modern life, together with medical, economic, and biological factors involved.

Estimate the proportion of divorces and broken families in a county, which are caused either by minor disagreements and maladjustments or because of lack of mutual consideration in sex matters.

XIV. *Three Problem Children.* One of the best and most concrete studies in the field of mental and social hygiene recently made is one made by the Joint Committee on the Prevention of Delinquency. This study was financed by the Commonwealth Fund, was one of several similar studies, and was published under the title *Three Problem Children*. Here are illustrated both problems and methods.

How many "Problem" children have come to your attention within the year, and how would you classify them?

XV. *Social Waste.* The 1926 North Carolina Conference for Social Service took for its subject "North Carolina's Social Deficit," keeping in mind the efforts of the state government toward its financial deficits and surplus. For the next year the Conference will discuss and study "North Carolina's Social Resources." Between these two extremes the chasm widens largely because of North Carolina's "social waste." In town, in city, on farms, in institutions, how much waste in childhood, womanhood, education, crime, poverty, undeveloped farms, run down landscapes, must be noticed?

List a score of items in which social waste might be prevented by good social work.

# CHAPTER V

## PROBLEMS OF CHILD WELFARE AND DEVELOPMENT

*A Little Child Shall Lead Them.* With the prophetic "And a little child shall lead them" was ushered in a new era of social study, social work, and educational practice. Of course, the importance of the child has never changed, but the recognition of the organic meaning to the whole of society and humanity is a later development. In the old historical days many approaches were made to the subject, and one of the old great books of wisdom held "That the world is saved only by the breath of the school children," while the Christian era ushered in the other recognition, "Of such is the kingdom." Nevertheless, for many generations the social tragedy of the world has been the tragedy of childhood.

*Child Welfare.* In the Modern era the child welfare part of social work has predominated, and it has advanced simultaneously alongside the great new era of the child-emphasis in education, psychology, and social practice. There is yet much coördination to be done between the two great branches of child welfare involved in the field of social work and education, but there is much promise in this field, as has been pointed out in the discussion of the training for leadership in social work. The questions in this chapter are based on *Problems of Child Welfare* by Mangold.

157. What is child welfare?
158. What are the social obligations to childhood?

*The Conservation of Life.* (Chapters 1, 2, 3, 4, 5, 6, 7.) A special phase of child welfare which is engaging the attention of students of society is that of the relation of the number of children to the total population, to the health and stamina of individuals and society, and to the whole problem of the death rate and general health of children everywhere. One of the most important methods of increasing population is the reduction of the death rate among children. The following questions are of importance:

159. What may be called a reasonable increase in population?
160. How does the fecundity of the American mother compare with that of the foreign born?

161. What are the causes of the declining birth-rate?

162. What has been the reason for the gradually increasing expectation of life of the inhabitants of our Western nations?

163. In general, to what factors can New Zealand's low infant mortality rate be attributed?

164. What is the median age at death of measles, whooping cough, diphtheria?

165. How has death rate from diphtheria been reduced?

166. What are the so-called diseases of early infancy?

167. According to the analysis by the Children's Bureau, what are the causes of death by diseases of early infancy? digestive diseases? respiratory diseases?

168. How are they preventable?

169. What are the two methods of providing good milk for children?

170. Explain pasteurization.

171. What has been the result of the milk code in New York City as far as infant mortality is concerned?

172. Discuss fully the function of the welfare center.

173. What is the relation of mortality and overcrowding?

174. How have European countries solved the

problem of the large mortality rate of infants born to working mothers?
175. Discuss the problem of the midwife.
176. What are the important provisions of the New York City laws in regard to the midwife?
177. How has the federal government aided maternity and infant work?

*Health and Physique.* (Chapters 7, 8, 9, 10, 11.) In the previous chapter the whole problem of health in its relation to social disorganization was discussed. In this chapter specific phases of health in relation to child welfare will be presented in special questions. Here, again, not only physical health but mental and social health are important. Here enters one of the most important of modern social prophylaxes as found in the newer philosophy of play and recreation. So important is this phase of social development that Professor Ross has even listed it as one of the major social products of society.

178. What are the effects of bad environment on physique of children? Discuss fully.
179. What are the more serious defects found among school children? The minor defects?

180. What is the present status of medical inspection and physical examination of school children?
181. What should be the program dealing with the pre-school child?
182. What provision should be made for the education of the blind, deaf, crippled?
183. Discuss the open air school.
184. What are the advantages of the school lunch room?
185. What is the function of the school nurse?
186. Explain the three theories of play.
187. Discuss fully the values of recreation.
188. What should be the facilities for recreation?
189. Why is supervision in play important?
190. Explain the boy scout movement—its history and aims.
191. Discuss the school as a social center.

*Training and Education.* (Chapters 12, 13, 14, 15, 16, 17.) One of the chief products of the newer emphasis on personality and social differences is the recognition of the importance of giving children individual attention in school, home, and community. Experience and the democratic experiment has also shown the importance of social means for guaranteeing that all the children of all the people have an opportunity for equal development. This brings in the question of compulsory school attendance and its attendant problems. It involves the whole question of inequality between town and city and the question of vocational guidance and education.

192. Give the most important causes of backwardness.
193. What is the system of classification used by the United States Bureau of Education in regard to mentally defective children?
194. What is the system of training for the feebleminded? the backward?
195. What has been done in the school for the exceptionally gifted child?
196. On what three groups does our high illiteracy rate depend?
197. Discuss briefly compulsory school attendance laws.
198. What is the Platoon System?
199. What steps have led to an improvement in rural education?
200. What are the functions of the school as a social service agency?
201. What is an ideal program of vocational education?
202. Explain the continuation school.
203. What are the recommendations of the special committee of the American Federation of Sex Hygiene in regard to sex instruction?

*Child Labor*. (Chapters 18, 19, 20, 21.) Within recent years no phase of the child welfare problem has been discussed in public more than the problem of child labor. This has been brought about by the continuous agitation for an amendment to the Federal Constitution. This amendment was defeated by more than three-fourths of the states of the union. On both sides the propaganda methods illustrated the lack of common-sense and scientific procedure in the search after adequate social legislation. While the question of the amendment is apparently now a dead one, there is an increasing earnestness and emphasis on all sides to see that each state shall do its part in the prevention of child labor in its domain. It is important that the problem be approached more earnestly and more scientifically.

204. Discuss the chief causes of child labor as given by Mangold.
205. How have modern industrial conditions influenced child labor?
206. Discuss the child in the street trades— newspaper selling, errand and delivery work.
207. Discuss compulsory education as a child labor law.
208. What are the minimum standards of

children entering employment as estab-
lished at the Child Welfare Conference in
1919?
209. Discuss the employment certificate system (working papers).
210. Briefly, what is status of child labor legislation in this country?

*Juvenile Delinquency.* (Chapters 22, 23, 24, 25,
26.) Juvenile delinquency and the juvenile court
have assumed increasingly large proportions in
the whole field of social work and public welfare
within recent years. Here have been recognized
age long injustices. Here has been developed an
important phase of social work—which ties in
effectively with the modern youth movement.
Here is great promise of the future, but also opportunity for better study.

211. What are the conditions underlying
juvenile delinquency?
212. Explain juvenile court—type of case
handled, hearing, treatment, and disposition of offender.
213. What are the qualifications of a juvenile
judge?
214. Why is the probation system called the
keystone of the juvenile court?
215. What is usual length of probation?

216. Explain the following: detention home; parental school; industrial school; republic.
217. Give brief description of the cottage system.
218. What are contributory delinquency laws?
219. Mention important measures of child protection.

*Problems of Dependent Children.* (Chapters 27, 28, 29, 30, 31.) Perhaps the most popular of the old approaches to child welfare was that of the dependent child. Here was a problem which demanded and received recognition and sympathy. But in no phase of child welfare has there been more radical change in methods. The recognition by social workers and workers of all the professions of the importance of the home has not always been consistently developed and practiced. There has been, however, a very definite trend away from the old idea of placing all dependent children in orphanages and homes to the definite practice of giving them foster homes or of planning for institutions to approach conditions of the family.

220. Give types of dependents.
221. Give most important principles asserted at the White House Conference.
222. How is coöperation promoted between child caring agencies?

223. Discuss the need for reform in regard to the illegitimate child.
224. What is the Minnesota law?
225. What are Home and Aid Societies?
226. Give standards to be observed in placing children in private homes.
227. What are the results of the placing-out system?
228. What are the advantages of the institution?
229. Discuss the State School System.
230. What are the disadvantages of the subsidy system?
231. What are the principal features of the mothers' Pension Laws?
232. What is the service rendered by the various code commissions?
233. Discuss the work of the United States Children's Bureau.
234. Mention other agencies whose primary object is child welfare.

SPECIAL QUESTIONS FOR STUDY AND ILLUSTRATION

XVI. *The Rural Child*. In the field of education it is often pointed out that the school facilities of the rural child are not so good as those of the city. The rural child may have a shorter term with poorer facilities while his city cousin benefits by longer terms and better facilities. Is this true also in the general field of social welfare? How about nutrition and health? How about recreation and play? How about vocational training and opportunities?

List ways in which rural boys and girls are handicapped in a given county.

XVII. *Mothers' Aid.* Miss Emith Tuttle, of the North Carolina State Board of Charities and Public Welfare, has recently completed a study of mothers' aid work in that state. She has gathered together cases and problems and shown how important this long neglected field is. Among other important principles involved is the one that children ought to be allowed to remain at home with mothers rather than be placed in institutions, wherever this can be done in normal homes.

Recalling all of your experience, list every case of a child being sent to an institution because of poverty in the home of a widowed mother?

XVIII. *Whose Fault?* In one of the communities of a North Carolina county which had not had the benefit of mothers' aid there was recently reported in the papers the case of a mother who committed suicide. Her husband had died a few years pre-

viously.  Her children were growing up
and she and they, so far as seemed
possible, were working in a factory.  But
the struggle seemed too hard.

Of course there were circumstances
complicating this, as all other situations.
But whose fault was this tragedy?  Explain various angles of possible plans for
helping in cases like this.

XIX. *School Attendance.*  Dr. Sloop tells about
some instances in which parents whom
she prosecuted for not sending their
children to school later became her good
friends.  A superintendent of public welfare relates that two of the fathers whom
she had prosecuted once helped her pull
her Ford out of the mud and offered to
go all the way to town with her to avoid
further similar mishap.  Another invited
her to dinner.  She had made her case
clear to them.

Illustrate how through good work the
parents may be made to see the importance of school without prosecution.

XX. *Children   Astray.*  The   Harvard   University Press has recently issued a large,
handsome  volume  under  the  title  of
*Children  Astray.*  Many  other  volumes
and  articles  have  recently  been  published to help out in the whole problem of

the maladjusted boy and girl, and to help parents to understand and to perform their tasks better.

Classify the "children astray" within your own knowledge according to causes. What "plans" for bringing them back can you offer?

# CHAPTER VI

## HUMAN FACTORS IN INDUSTRY AND AGRICULTURE

*Labor not Merely a Commodity.* Among the many emphatic statements made by President Wilson, dealing with the principles and philosophy of democracy, was one in which he reiterated with great clearness and force the statement that human labor was not merely a commodity. This truth, of course, has been recognized in increasing degree over a long period of time. Nevertheless, it has constantly needed re-emphasis from the changing viewpoints of social and industrial leaders. In Chapter III some of the problems of industry were discussed, and in Chapter IV some of the problems of maladjustment due to industrial situations were presented. One division of this chapter deals with some of the more practical phases of the human relationships in industry. This division is an approach to the whole field of social work and industrial relations. The other is the much neglected field of the human factors in rural life and agriculture. Questions on the first topic will be based upon *The Human Factor in Industry* by Frankel and Fleisher, published by the Macmillan Company. There is no volume dealing adequately with the human factors in tenant farming, or any other important rural relationships, but Fiske's *The Challenge of the Country*, published by the Association Press, gives an excellent interpretation of the spirit and possibilities of country life.

*The Problem of the Industrial Misfit.* (Chapters 1, 2, 3, 4.) Mathew Arnold's much quoted statement about the blessedness of the man who has found his work might well be applied to this new era of restlessness in a machine age, although it is manifestly impossible to insure a social and industrial order in which each individual will surely love his work. Too much emphasis can not be put upon the effort to make all possible adjustments between the individual and his work. There has arisen, therefore, important techniques through which misfits may be diminished, the labor turnover reduced, and an increasing amount of harmony produced.

235. What are the four phases of employment?
236. Describe the employment machinery of an effective organization.

237. What are the methods of securing a good supply of workers?
238. What is meant by hiring and holding?
239. What are the four considerations which determine the desirability of a job?
240. What are the four essentials of the good worker?
241. What sort of employment records ought to be kept?
242. What is the purpose of a physical examination?
243. What are the evidences of the need of industrial education?
244. How is vocational training more needed than formerly?
245. Discuss part-time schools.
246. Discuss the coöperation of public schools with industry.
247. What are the qualifications of a teacher of vocational education?
248. Give illustrations of the types of training for industrial workers.
249. Discuss the need for general education on the part of the workers.
250. What is meant by cultural classes?
251. Discuss education for leisure time.

*Health and Working Conditions.* (Chapters 5, 6, 7, 9.) A picture of the modern industrial plant compared with the varied types of earlier days shows marked contrast. In addition to the general recognition of the rights and personality of the worker in general philosophy, great strides have been made in improving working conditions in factory, shop, and mill. Changes in the number of working hours, in health conditions, in safety devices, in social enjoyment, in democratic participation in industry, have all marked this advance. Nevertheless, conditions are far from satisfactory now, either to the worker or employee. Continuous study, therefore, must be depended upon to bring about further results.

252. Discuss recent change in attitude towards working hours.
253. What is the relation of fatigue to efficiency and happiness on the part of the worker?
254. Discuss causes and remedies of fatigue.
255. How measure fatigue?
256. Discuss the shorter working day as a measure of economy.
257. Discuss night work.
258. Discuss over-time and Sunday work.
259. What is the best "normal" working period?
260. Discuss vacation periods.
261. What are some of the important advances in working conditions?
262. Discuss safety devices and methods.

263. Outline methods of preventing occupational diseases.
264. Outline a satisfactory standard for sanitation.
265. What are the general principles of lighting?
266. Discuss standards and methods of ventilation.
267. Outline newer methods of fire protection.
268. Discuss the whole problem of illness and industrial efficiency.
269. What are some of the methods of health protection in industry?
270. Discuss medical examinations.
271. What are some of the medical equipment requirements of a good plant?
272. What sort of clinics are practicable?
273. Discuss the special diseases in industry.
274. What sort of health records should be kept?
275. Outline a course of lectures on health education.
276. What are some of the ways of increasing social life pleasures among employees?
277. What are the advantages of lunch rooms and cafeterias?
278. Outline plans for rest and recreation rooms.
279. Discuss typical noon and evening hours' diversion.
280. Give illustration of recreation equipment.
281. List a dozen types of play and recreation.

*The Employer and Social Welfare.* (Chapters 8, 10, 11, 12.) Fundamental in the whole process of industrial social welfare are the questions of wages, the attitude of the employer, participation by the employee in the control of industry, and the organization of all matters relating to labor and labor welfare. The question of wages is one of unceasing debate. Shall it be based upon output, or upon capacity, upon standard of living, upon family needs, or what? What are some of the ways of supplementing wages? What are the merits of "welfare work," and of paternalistic measures? These and many other questions which follow need to be studied carefully:

282. Give a definition of wages.
283. What are some of the methods of fixing the wage rate?
284. What is meant by time and piece-work wages?
285. Discuss other methods of payment.
286. What are the stimuli besides money that may be offered?
287. Illustrate profit sharing as the solution of the wage problem.
288. Discuss coöperation of employers and employees.

289. Discuss the whole problem of industrial housing.
290. What are the advantages and disadvantages of company owned houses?
291. Discuss the importance of town planning.
292. State the standards for a single family house.
293. What are some of the community activities of an industrial community?
294. Discuss methods of insurance among employees.
295. What types of insurance may be offered?
296. Discuss old age pensions.
297. What is the importance of savings and loans?
298. List a half-dozen methods of coöperative savings?
299. Outline an effective organization for department of labor in an effective industry.

*The Farmer and His Work.* Because of the rapid industrialization and urbanization of society in the last century, the social problems of labor in industry have become so complex as to overshadow still other important relationships as found in country life and on the farm. It is true that the study of rural sociology has developed into a considerable movement, but the human factors in the farmer's work, in the tenant's labor, and in

varied other agricultural pursuits have been made
secondary to the general statistical discussion of
the agricultural output. The student of social
problems and the social worker ought not to
forget the distinctive relationships and situations
in which the farmer and his family, the owner and
his helper must find happiness, interest, and
profit.

*The Rural Problem.* (Chapters 1, 2, 3.) The
picturesque phases of country life have continuously been portrayed in literature and art.
The sturdiness of rural character has been exalted,
the history of America has been the history of
leadership developed from rural homes. Nevertheless, so rapidly has grown the industrial and
urban civilization, as well as changes in ideals and
standards, that the work of the farmer too often
has come to be considered an inferior task.

300. What, after all, is the rural problem?
301. Contrast the growth of cities and the de-
pletion of the country.
302. What are some of the evidences of rural
decadence?
303. How many rural communities do you know
that are less prosperous than they were
twenty years ago?

304. Why do you believe in the bigness of rural life?
305. Criticize the country boy's creed?
306. Discuss some of the attractive features of living in the country.
307. What is the country life movement?
308. Why is the problem of leadership in the rural community so important?
309. What are some agencies for the development of a better farm life?
310. What will be the effect of the automobile and radio upon the new rural life?

*Opportunities for the Future.* (Chapters 4, 5.) It is commonly retorted to those who urge the farmer to remain and take delight in the country, that, first of all, he must be assured of a living. Agriculture, they say, must be made to pay, and there must be zest and joy in a rural social order. There must be, they insist, a place in which he can be assured of raising his family under as good circumstances as in the city.

311. What is meant by scientific agriculture?
312. Why is the farmer so prejudiced against newer developments?
313. What are the handicaps in the South to intensive farming?

314. Is the farmer more individualistic than the city man?
315. Discuss the difficulties of organizing farmers.
316. Illustrate lack of coöperation in business and education.
317. Discuss the lack of play life in the rural community.
318. What is meant by rural socialization?

*Education and Leadership.* The most common complaint about country life is the fact that its leaders have gone. Those who are left are either poor leaders or bad leaders. Those who are being trained are being trained in the methods of industrial and urban leadership. The country, therefore, suffers. Rural education has in no wise been equal to city education, and consequently the country boy and girl have not fared equally with their city cousin.

319. Discuss some weaknesses and limitations of the country school.
320. Discuss a modern rural school, and its part in developing the human factors in agriculture.
321. What is meant by rural Christian forces?
322. What is meant by old and new church ideals?

323. What is meant by Christian states-
manship?
324. Discuss the need for the rural doctor.

SPECIAL QUESTIONS FOR STUDY AND ILLUSTRATION

XXI. *Difficult Situations*. Many enthusiastic
students of industrial relations set a hard
task for society and human nature when
they demand that every worker must
be provided with work which he enjoys
with zestful anticipation. Neither the
physiology of growth, nor the vicissitudes
of age and sex and race would make this
likely to the perfect degree suggested.
Nor would the psychological principles
underlying growth and development be
met if there were no difficulties of struggle
or drive. Nevertheless, there ought to
be considerably more effort put forth to
adjust worker and work.

Classify two score workers who seem
clearly to be misfits in their work, and
suggest remedies.

XXII. *A New Industrial Community*. There
are those who have prophesied that the
Piedmont South, extending from Birmingham, through Atlanta, North Georgia,
the Carolinas, and Virginia would develop a newer type of village industrial
community conducive to democratic life

and development. Why follow in the wake of all past mistakes? Others have been afraid that such communities would not develop into democratic communities.

What are the social problems involved in a mill community which are different from those back home from whence the workers came?

XXIII. *The Tenant and His Work.* Throughout the United States there have been many studies of tenancy and much fear lest the farm owning civilization of America might deteriorate. In the South there is the double problem of white and negro tenants. In social work and education the problem is a critical one because of many factors of community leadership and development.

Compare all cases of crime, dependency, and defectiveness in a given area and classify according to farm ownership.

# CHAPTER VII

## COMMUNITY ORGANIZATION AND PUBLIC WELFARE ADMINISTRATION

*Community Responsibility.* In all efforts for adjusting human relationships the community responsibility is large. Social deficiencies and social problems are invariably closely linked up with the community process in both cause and effect. The war and its emergency social work and emergency organization revealed the possibilities of community organization as an effective force. Allowing for wide differences of objectives and methods in war times and in peace, there were nevertheless many lessons to be learned from efforts toward community organization. There has arisen, therefore, a concerted movement looking towards more effective community organization and more study of the problem. The most complete story of the community organization movement is that given by Professor J. F. Steiner, of the University of North Carolina, in his volume, *Community Organization*, just published by the Century Company. The questions in this chapter are based upon his volume.

*The Community Movement and Social Progress.*
(Chapters 1, 2, 3, 4, 5, 6.)   The history of communities, like the history of families, of nations, and of movements, provides much rich material for the study of social organization.   Communities and community consciousness evolve and vary in accordance with the differing stages of civilization and culture.   The new study of social psychology has accentuated group study of the community and has set in motion many efforts to study group consciousness.

325. Discuss briefly the growth of group consciousness.
326. How has the scientific study of social problems made possible the modern community movement?
327. Explain—associate community, federate community, neighborhood.
328. Give at least two classifications of types of communities.
329. Define social disorganization.   What does it entail?
330. How may sectarianism be a disorganizing force in the community?
331. Give characteristics of provincial community solidarity.
332. How may community solidarity be attained?

333. Under what circumstances may community solidarity retard social progress?
334. How may custom interfere with community progress? Illustrate.
335. How may a crisis lead to community progress?
336. What institutions of a community are most likely to be dominated by a conservative spirit?
337. How may this attitude be overcome?
338. Explain fully how the problem of community change is affected by economic factors.

*Typical Experiments in Community Organization.* (Chapters 7, 8, 9, 10, 11, 12, 13, 14, 15, 16, 17, 18, 19.) After all, there is no better way to understand a movement, to find its strong and weak points, or to undertake its utilization than the study of typical experiments. In the field of community organization, no less than elsewhere, there have been many changes in policy and practice.

339. What three methods stand out in the promotion of relief coördination?
340. What has been the influence of the Charity Organization Movement on community organization?

341. Give distinctive features of the settlement movement.
342. How does it differ from the charity organization movement?
343. How has the settlement influenced the community movement?
344. Use the South Park System of Chicago as an example in a discussion of neighborhood organization.
345. Give briefly history and purpose of organization of Community Service (Incorporated).
346. In what way has the contribution of the playground and recreation movement to community organization been limited?
347. Give briefly a history of the Rochester experiment in the wider use of school buildings.
348. What are the necessary provisions of a law adequate to enable growth of this movement?
349. What is the nature of community center activities?
350. What have been the two problems in the history of agriculture?
351. Which one was brought out by the Country Life Commission in 1908?
352. Give briefly a history of the country life movement.
353. What are some of the problems in rural organization?

354. Explain the Farm Bureau plan of organization, the Rural Community Council.
355. Explain nature and purpose of Central Council of Social Agencies.
356. Explain the organization of the financial federation in Detroit.
357. What are the principles of the financial federation movement?
358. Explain the work of the Cleveland Foundation.
359. How is the Survey a means of community organization?
360. What is the principle generally and advantageously adopted in community surveys as to method used in discovering facts? Explain.
361. Explain case history of a community.
362. How can a church deserve the name community church?
363. What is the federated church?
364. What are the limitations of the community church movement?
365. Discuss Home Service of the American Red Cross—origin and entrance into community work.
366. Discuss the county plan of organization as one of its contributions.
367. Give briefly its advantages and disadvantages as a community agency.
368. Give the outstanding features of the Social

Unit Organization as worked out in Cincinnati.

369. Define industrial welfare work.

370. Explain organization of a mining community, Southern mill village.

371. Give reasons for failure of organization at Pullman.

372. What is public welfare?

373. Give the county organization plan of North Carolina.

374. What is the significance of the Public Welfare movement in community organization?

375. Give distinguishing features of the Cincinnati Federation, Boston Health League, and Cleveland Health Federation.

376. Explain State Councils of Social Agencies as exemplified by Ohio.

377. In general, what is the influence of national organizations on local community organization?

378. What is the purpose of the National Social Work Council?

379. What has been done in the field of co-ordinating national health agencies?

380. Why is such coördination important?

*Theories and Principles of Community Organization.* (Chapters 20, 21, 22, 23, 24, 25.) Growing out of the experience of the community, and of its many leaders, there has developed a considerable body of expert evidence from which may be drawn certain conclusions. Some of these conclusions justify tentative theories and principles of community organization. If good social theory may be termed a workable blueprint for social progress, may we not hope that some of these theories of community organization may point the way to happier and more effective social relationships?

381. What is central thought of community organization?
382. Of what does it consist?
383. Give the six theories under which may be grouped various experiments in community organization.
384. Explain briefly these theories.
385. In what way should the community organization movement be a protest against the crowd spirit?
386. In light of above, explain why the Cincinnati Social Unit Organization is rendering good service in building up a community program.
387. What is the newer view of community organization?
388. Give briefly a summary of principles that should govern community organization.

389. Why are thorough community studies essential to successful community organization?
390. How has the community movement been handicapped by lack of trained leadership?
391. What is meant by apprentice method of training in the field of social work?
392. What is newer conception?
393. What schools have laid emphasis upon education for community work?

SPECIAL QUESTIONS FOR STUDY AND ILLUSTRATIONS

XXIV. *The State System of Public Welfare·* The administration of social work agencies under the auspices of government involves a number of special features not found in private and voluntary agencies. An interesting exercise would be to compare the growth and development of education from private and denominational to state auspices with the similar process going on in public welfare.

What lessons may be learned from this comparison between public welfare administration with public education?

XXV. *The County as A Unit of Social Work.* Another profitable comparison with education will be found in the county unit of administration. In most of the

state systems the rule is, of course, to
have a county superintendent of schools
in charge of the county schools and
sometimes coördinating with the towns
as well. What are the conditions, if
any, which make a county superintendent of schools in every county more
essential than a county superintendent
of public welfare?

Is equal opportunity for normal development in the child any more a matter of
"charity" than equal opportunity to
go to school?

XXVI. Still a third comparison may be made
with the administration of the county
system of public education. The county
superintendent of schools has charge
of the country schools while the city
superintendents take charge of the city
schools? Under what conditions do
counties have the county unit for both
town and country?

Under what circumstances would you
recommend the town or city having a
special system of public welfare?

XXVII. *Systems of Public Welfare.* There is a
brief summary of many types of organization for public welfare in the little
manual, *Systems of Public Welfare,* prepared by Howard W. Odum and D. W.

Willard and published by the University of North Carolina Press. Chapters are devoted to state systems, county systems, and city systems, and they may be studied for general reference.

What are the difficulties involved in each of the types of administration—state, county, city?

XXVIII. *Administering Social Work in the Small Community.* An important meeting of the 1926 National Conference of Social work was devoted to the consideration of the small community and its problem of social work. The meeting was unusually well attended and developed a most commendable interest and enthusiasm. Nevertheless, there seems to be almost unanimity of opinion that little has been evolved of permanent value in this field.

What are the peculiar problems of the small community with reference to its social work and social work agencies?

# CHAPTER VIII

## NORTH CAROLINA AS A COMPOSITE FIELD OF SOCIAL WORK AND PUBLIC WELFARE

*An Example of Analysis.* This chapter will attempt to present a single state as an example of the field and opportunity for social work and public welfare. North Carolina, because of its recent legislation in public welfare, its experimental efforts in organization and administration, its plan for advance in the whole field of education, public health and social welfare, and its difficult situations involved in rural areas, offers an excellent example for study. Other states may be studied in similar ways, while excellent projects in the field of study and experiment may also be found in individual counties and cities. This chapter, of course, will only sketch in outline opportunities and problems. At most it will present briefly a simple analysis of the situation with its promise and its limitations. Although the story of North Carolina in no wise gives an example of a system which coördinates social work agencies and resources effectively, the keynote of this chapter and the outlook for the state is a hopeful one. Among the reasons which may be assigned for hopefulness in the North Carolina experiment are the general facts that the state is fully aware that the experiment has only begun, that as yet it has yielded only little definite final value, but that there is ample evidence to indicate a good beginning. Furthermore, the North Carolina plan is peculiarly well adapted to social development of a rural state, and it approaches the whole problem of the social work part of government in definite and concrete ways.

*The North Carolina Plan of Public Welfare.* Perhaps the first point of emphasis should be that the North Carolina Plan provides preëminent emphasis on rural social work. No one, I believe, will challenge adequately the statement that rural social work has never yet been successfully done. Whether a county unit plan such as North Carolina has provided in connection with its governmental public welfare can become the basis for utilizing all resources, coördinating efforts, finding personnel, and adapting itself to the much needed tasks will depend upon a number of factors, some of which will be enumerated subsequently. North Carolina has one hundred counties. Each county with a population of 32,000 or more is required to employ a county superintendent of public welfare. He is elected jointly by the county commissioners and the county board of education. As an advisory group there is a county board of public welfare of three in each county. A state-wide juvenile court act creates a juvenile court in each county with the clerk of superior court as judge. In counties having populations of less than 32,000 the superintendent of schools may serve in the capacity of superintendent of public welfare where no full-time superintendent of public welfare is elected. The county unit system is a part of the statewide plan of the State Board of Charities and Public Welfare which performs its work through a Commissioner of Public Welfare and bureaus of County Organization, Child Welfare, Institutions, Mental Health and Hygiene, Negro Work, Promotion and Publicity. In turn, there is a similar general division of activities of the county superintendents including county administration and coöperation with State Board, general child welfare work, charities and corrections, probation and juvenile court work, school attendance work, community organization, and recreation. The large problem of school attendance work, while limiting the activities of the superintendent of public welfare towards community organization and coördination may, nevertheless, become an admirable basis for coöperative efforts in child welfare and family case work.

*Special Difficulties.* Difficult problems which the North Carolina plan faces are many. In addition to the usual problems involved in rural situations with sparsely settled areas, isolation, bad roads, undeveloped attitudes towards social work, limited personnel, resources, and uninformed leadership, there are other problems to be faced. How coördinate other social work agencies and voluntary groups in the county? How effect cordial coöperation between town and country? How bring about both intelligently planned and executed work and coöperation on the part of social worker and farm and home demonstration agent, public health nurse, county physician, schools and teachers, churches and social service, national social work organizations? How bring about effective social work and public welfare among Negroes? How interpret public welfare as the social work part of government? How overcome the elements of limited training and political habits? How, finally, make social work and public welfare the great process of discovery, interpretation, adaptation, and leadership so essential in rural communities?  Can the county be a county unit, or will it be only an approximate substitute for a unit?  Will there be parallel systems and efforts in town and country?  Will each of the separate workers in public welfare, voluntary social work, home and farm demonstration, public health, as technician perform badly only a part of the work?

*Seven Years of Experiment.*  The basis of the present North Carolina plan of public welfare is found in the legislation of 1919 with minor amendments in 1921.  To what extent has North Carolina succeeded during these seven years, first in terms of actual numerical efforts, and second in terms of the larger beginnings?  The last report of the Commissioner of Public Welfare shows that although only twenty-nine counties are required by law there were, nevertheless, fifty-five counties which had appointed superintendents of public welfare.  Numerically, therefore, the showing is very creditable.  There has been also a steady growth in the amount of work done and a constant improvement in its quality.  There has developed, too, a steady professional spirit among

the county superintendents of public welfare and
continuous improvement in their qualifications
and methods.    They now have a statewide organization which meets annually with the Institutes of
Public Welfare held at the University under the
auspices of the Commissioner of Public Welfare
and the University School of Public Welfare.
For six years these Institutes have been held each
summer with increasing effectiveness and with an
average attendance of more then fifty.    During
the last two years the commissioner has provided
regular lecture courses and examinations and has
given certificates to superintendents completing
the work.    The superintendents themselves have
joined in suggesting that standards of certification be set, and that ideals be raised higher and
higher.    During the 1926 Institute the program
provided not only for the regular lectures, but also
for a continuation course to extend throughout the
year as a follow-up to the main divisions of study at
the Institutes and work in the state and county
departments.

The fact that the number of counties employ-
ing superintendents of public welfare has been
continuously on the increase, and that such variations and fluctuations as have occurred have not

affected the general progress of public welfare is an acknowledged asset.  An important factor in the development of public opinion both in the State at large and in certain counties has been the enthusiasm and influence of the State Federation of Women's Clubs, the League of Women Voters, and other women's organizations.  A large number of concrete attainments might be cited as evidence that the North Carolina plan has achieved substantial and successful beginnings.

*Marked Limitations.*  Nevertheless, it must be admitted that up to the present time there has been no county organized successfully on anything like a complete or satisfactory basis.  There has been no county organization which has ample personnel and resources.  There has been no county in which the work of town and rural areas has been adequately correlated.  There has been no county with a satisfactory permanently going county council.  There has been no county in which the work of the superintendent of public welfare has met the wishes and standards of all other social work agencies.  There has been no county in which the county board of public welfare has functioned with complete satisfaction to all concerned.  There has been no county in which the home demonstration community clubs, the work of the farm demonstration agent, the public health nurse, and the school folk have been satisfactorily correlated. There is no county in which rural case work can be satisfactorily demonstrated. There is no county which the School of Public Welfare can use as a satisfactory type of field work. In other words, for the purposes of demonstrating a type of county unit of all social work such as would illustrate community organization, community councils, community chests, and other technical and theoretical aspects of the work, there is no North Carolina county which can be cited even as a reasonable example of success.

*Promising Features.* It must not be understood, however, from this that there are not outstanding examples of excellent work or that there are not now many nuclei upon which may be built in the near future more successful organizations. The very statements of limitations and of the partial achievements are but added to make of the county unit plan a more exemplary form of organization upon which to build rural social work of the future. A few examples may be cited. One county has this year, through the coöperation of the State Board of Charities and

Public Welfare and the Four-County Demonstration work in public welfare, made remarkable strides. A new superintendent of public welfare has been elected, a new probation officer—full-time man, graduate of the University—has been appointed, a supervisor of case work and a regular case worker have been utilized, a full-time Negro social worker has been employed, and the assistance of the head of the Bureau of work among negroes has been utilized continuously. In addition to this, a teacher social-worker has been employed by the Superintendent of Schools, and she has experimented with truancy cases and other cases alongside the work of the Superintendent of Public Welfare. She is a trained worker with the master's degree from the University of North Carolina. There have been also meetings in the city in which countywide invitations were extended; there have been successful efforts to establish a detention home for children; and in many ways beginnings have been made to interpret public welfare to the county.

*A Mountain County.* In another county, a typical mountain community, there has been developed one of the most successful demonstrations of public welfare possibilities in recent

years.   This plan was initiated from the coöperative efforts of the local folks and the Commissioner of Public Welfare.   The first steps were the
preliminary weeks of residence and organization
by the supervisor from the State Board of Charities and Public Welfare and two young women
from the School of Public Welfare.   Following
the preliminary months, one of these was elected
Superintendent of Public Welfare and has since
developed an admirable illustration of what can
be done in a limited and practical way.   She has
had the coöperation of the State Board and has
exemplified to some extent the possibilities of the
general utility social work leader in a county community which has not hitherto been acquainted
with professional social work.   She has helped
the people to understand social work.   She has
coöperated with farmers, with school folk, with
courthouse officials, and has become in a single
year a popular woman of the county.   The
chief point of emphasis here is the fact that the
work has been done well on the limited basis for
which it claims results.

*Other Types.*   Other very interesting types of
successful county public welfare work may be
found in the State.   One county has experimented

as a member of the community chest and has made numerous efforts at coördinating work of county and town. Other counties in many ways become admirable examples of successful interpretation of the whole problem of public welfare to the county. Their mothers' aid work, and their general community organization are examples of the type of approach which may well net complete county organization in the future. Still another county has demonstrated a really successful experiment in community organization through countywide recreation programs and special days. Many other counties have excelled in special efforts, such as undernourished children, special health work, and social hygiene,—illustrating the possibilities of public health nurse as social worker, tuberculosis prevention, Negro work, a real juvenile court organization and special efforts in adult education, special efforts in probation work and countywide recreation clubs, and coördination with the churches. A number of counties are object lessons in persistence, quiet devotion to work, with superintendents who have stood by from the beginning of the state system. A number of counties have typified the difficulties of the trained worker in adapting himself to rural areas and the complications of politics and lack of understanding.

*The Outlook.* A review of the seven years' work and of the evidence in hand will make clear, of course, the basis for the almost uniform skepticism of the professional social worker in the United States as to the effectiveness of the North Carolina plan. From his viewpoint and from the viewpoint of the city technique and the traditional specialisms of social work his skepticism is undoubtedly justified. The county system has not succeeded. But passing over the absurdity of any system of this sort succeeding in so short a while, his skepticism and criticisms are but a stimulating challenge to those who are seeking a more effective mode of social work for rural areas and a better technique for social work as a part of government. A reasonable attitude seems to be one of satisfaction that the plan is available, that certain beginnings have been made, that many of the difficulties in the way have been at least interpreted, that many of the first dangers have been overcome, that the difficulties are not underestimated, and that there is no disillusionment as to how much has, or has not been accomplished. The system does not accept the premise that success comes only through any provincial type of community organization or specialized technique, standards for which are admittedly not uniformly accepted and are undergoing radical changes at the present time. The value of the plan will therefore be found in its success in working out means, methods, and resources suitable to its purposes and tasks, in which case its technique might be an object lesson for the future development of rural social work.

*Study and Research.* If, then, the county unit plan in North Carolina has in no sense demonstrated successful coördination of social work, and if at the same time it is paradoxically set up as an experiment of great promise, what are the considerations through which these conflicting judgments may be reconciled? Aside from the time element, and assuming the constants and variables which have been ever present in all new movements for social work and education, what are some of the principles and tasks which must occupy the attention and efforts of social work for the next decade? And, assuming the normal growth and progress along present and traditional lines, what are added features which must be worked out?

The first task is manifestly one of study and research, although in many cases problems of research must go hand in hand with problems of experiment, which is the second large task ahead.

There is perhaps no greater need now than that of finding out a proper technique of approach to adult population of rural areas in matters of social work and in subjects and problems involving different standards and social conflict. Recently I was much interested to hear one of the most experienced specialists in rural work among the churches in the United States complain bitterly of the failure of ministers and social workers in rural areas within his church domain. I have found unanimous agreement with this sentiment among social workers in mountain areas and extremely rural regions. But is the fault all the fault of the country folk? Our specialists admit that the major trend of the times is for the more energetic and better educated folk of the rural areas to move into cities. There are left, then, the other groups who have manifestly limited leadership, while the technique of all of our own leadership is aimed at the city or more highly educated people who have left the country. Added to this is the almost universal missionary emphasis which ought never to be substituted for the scientific or social work keynote which is always essential to ultimate success. Some new studies proposed in the field of teaching adults matters related to social concern, therefore, ought to yield results in time.

*Fifteen Type Studies.* Other important studies to be made are numerous. Taking a county, for instance, there are the following fields in which something more must be known before any final conclusions can be reached:

1. Genetic studies of marginal families with all the varied possibilities and significance to social work programs and possibilities.

2. Comprehensive studies of the general topography and areas with suitable maps of roads, communities, and resources.

3. The plotting of centers of leadership and other community areas in these maps with adequate studies of leadership resources.

4. Intensive and concrete studies of special communities within the county.

5. Concrete and special studies of school attendance and school delinquency.

6. Special studies and mental tests of groups of children.

7. Special studies of health and dietary conditions and practices.

8. Special studies of preschool times of children in the country and their family relationships.

9. Special inquiries concerning home, school, and vocational adaptations and opportunities in the rural places.

10. Special studies of attitudes towards social work and coöperation and of organizations available for social work.

11. Special inquiries into resources for voluntary social work and leadership.

12. Special case work studies of rural families compared and contrasted with other standard case studies.

13. Special inquiries into matters of coöperation between superintendents of schools and superintendents of public welfare.

14. Special inquiries into matters of coöperation between superintendents of public welfare and county boards of public welfare, county public health agencies, and the voluntary agencies.

15. Special historical studies of all matters of public welfare in the county to discover traditional or other handicaps.

*Social Work and Experiment.* It is clear, however, that this is a long-time task and that all such inquiries should be made gradually with common sense and sympathetic study, and wherever possible in such way as to render actual service and promote the cause of social work and public welfare. The studies therefore will often require an experimental basis of social work schedules of inquiry. Among the experiments which ought to be inaugurated will be:

1. Special efforts to make contact with particular leaders, and special programs and methods of stimulating sentiment for social work and public welfare.

2. Special experiments in which the visiting teacher or the social work teacher, as assistant to the county superintendent or school, may bring about closer coördination between the two departments.

3. Special experiments in which the public health nurse may become general social worker.

4. Special experiments for coördinating the work of home and farm demonstration agents with the countywide program of social work.

5. Special experiments in which countywide organization of parent-teacher associations may center efforts upon the preschool child, utilizing agencies of public welfare, health, home demonstration.

6. Special experiments in child welfare to determine something of the relation between undernourishment, school, work, and conduct.

7. Special experiments with farm and home

demonstration agents and school teachers in vocational guidance and direction, in connection with juvenile delinquency.

8. Experiments in countywide community organization with special provisions for the small community.

9. More thorough experiments in case work, case supervision, and record keeping.

10. Special experiments in several counties for obtaining more effective and intelligent work on the part of the county board of public welfare.

11. A series of experiments for interpreting public welfare to countywide groups and especially to county commissioners and members of boards of education.

12. Special experiments in Negro public welfare.

13. Special experiments in the coördination of county public welfare and industrial social work.

14. A demonstration county in the mountain areas.

15. A demonstration county in the east Carolina sandhills.

16. A statewide plan of coöperation between the State Superintendent of Schools and the Commissioner of Public Welfare for coördinating community education, adult teaching, and school attendance work.

17. A state-wide demonstration for more effective state coöperation and supervision of many aspects of public welfare work.

*Training for Social Work.*  Growing out of the results of these studies and experiments will come, of course, certain larger conclusions, questions, recommendations, and the basis upon which the whole field of public welfare may be interpreted to the public.  Along with these studies and experiments must be provided, of course, field work and observation for students in training for social work.  This is, of course, a major difficulty and a major problem second to none in the list, but omitted from the above list of problems of study and experiment in order to give it a special emphasis in the whole problem and to separate it from local tasks.  It seems clear, therefore, that if the studies and experiments needed are to be worked out in a simple, slow, but continuous way the resources for training social workers must not only be utilized to a large extent in coöperation with the State Board of Charities and Public Welfare but that this important objective should not be lost sight of in planning methods and resources.  In this way the results of studies and experiments may be brought together and made usable not only to many counties and communities in the state, but for social work in general.

*The Larger Program.*  Thus it will be seen that

in the social work and public welfare programs and opportunities in North Carolina are represented in large measure the essential tasks and problems which have been outlined in this volume. A review, therefore, of a particular state not only gives emphasis to the importance of well-grounded study and planning, but gives an admirable basis upon which to try out in practical work the social theory studied. Here are general problems of citizenship and of social welfare. Here are varied problems of social pathology and social deficiency. Here in a state with the largest birth rate and lowest death rate in the union is great opportunity for child welfare. Here are all of the essentials and problems of rural social work. Here in a tremendously expanding industrial civilization are tests for the best of social study and industrial social work. Here are opportunities for social research and adult education. And here are ample needs and opportunities for the training of social workers.

SPECIAL QUESTIONS FOR STUDY AND ILLUSTRATIONS

XXIX. *State Supervision and Control.* This chapter has discussed North Carolina's experiment from the veiwpoint of county administration largely. There are other problems. Much might be said about the limitations of the state work in supervising and controlling institutions for the socially deficient.

What are the glaring examples of institutional negligence, if any, in the state within the last five years? Prisons, Chaingangs, County Homes, Children's Homes, and others?

XXX. *Examples of Worth.* Just as was the case in the several counties referred to as making concrete contributions in special fields, so there have been many notable examples of success in institutional work.

Illustrate with concrete examples the work of a county in relation to its county homes, district hospitals, chaingangs, county cottage at the Jackson Training School, or other types.

XXXI. *County Councils, Agencies, Coöperation.* A number of counties are on the eve of trying out certain new types of countywide organizations. These experiments are of the utmost importance and indicate the wide range of opportunity in a single state.

Draw up a new plan of coöperative work for a single county.

XXXII. *Coöperation with the County Superintendent of Schools.* There have been excellent examples of very close and happy coöperation between superintendents of public welfare and superintendents of schools. There have been examples of failure to coöperate so well.

List all the causes that have come under your observation as being of importance in this problem of coöperative work.

XXXIII. *The Community Teacher and Worker.* Sometimes it is very clear that there is more work to be done by both superintendents, of education and of public welfare, than is possible to be done. Take school attendance work, as an example. Is there not some way whereby there can be assistance here and at the same time promotion of harmonious coöperation?

How about this plan: a community teacher and social worker as assistant to each superintendent of schools, and a state supervisor of school attendance work in the State Department of Public Welfare?

XXXIV. *Wholesome Attitudes.* In the opinion of many observers much, perhaps the greater part, of the constant criticism

of social work and public welfare would
be eliminated or mitigated if the people
at large could understand that social
work has come to stay in the same sense
of permanency and effectiveness as
education. There would then be more
constructive criticism and coöperation.

What are neglected factors through
which public welfare work may be
interpreted to the people?

XXXV. *Other States and Other Systems.* Other
particulars of the North Carolina plan
may be studied by those not familiar.
Reports of the Commissioner of Public
Welfare, Mrs. Kate Burr Johnson, of
Raleigh, will give many added details,
while special bulletins and reports will
enrich the whole story.

Other states have different systems.
Virginia puts more emphasis upon the
local boards. Contrast the North
Carolina plan with other states and
note advantages and disadvantages.

# CHAPTER IX

## THE RAPIDLY GROWING CITY AS A PROB-
## LEM STUDY IN PUBLIC WELFARE
## AND SOCIAL WORK

*The Problem City as a Review and Summary.*
One of the best ways to test knowledge and practice is through concrete illustrations. The previous chapter was devoted to one state considered
in the light of a problem study, and with special
emphasis upon the county as a unit. In this
chapter may be found another type of problem
study as found in the rapidly growing city. Such
a chapter may serve as a supplement to the previous one, and also, to some extent, as a summary of
the entire "approach" to social work and public
welfare.

*The New City.* Here are problem cities grown
over night from country towns to urban proportions. Some owe their rapid rise to the development of manufacturing and industrial interests.
Others have appeared like magic cities, as tourists'
meccas, regional playgrounds, and realtors' happy
hunting grounds. Still others have drawn their
new life from the normal development of agricul-

tural areas, the utilization of newly discovered resources, or the incidence of advantageous situations. Some there are whose greater proportions arise out of the establishment of new governmental, educational, or other institutions. Besides these new cities suburban areas all over the land are growing up to add their quota of problems of changing relationships to the great American scene.

*Varied Problems of Social Relationships.* All of these cities and communities present similar problems of public welfare and social work. It is true that many concrete problems will be different in the several communities, but from the viewpoint of the administration of social work and public welfare,[1] they present many of the same difficulties of organization, interpretation, and scope. Rapid growth has brought a large increase in the number and variety of social problems and "cases" for social treatment. At the same time the energies and resources of the community, its individuals and its organizations, have been devoted to physical development to the general

[1] It should be kept constantly in mind that in this volume "public welfare" is a very definite term, and refers to the "social work" part of government.

neglect of social adjustments. This, of course, is but natural and almost inevitable. Nevertheless, it does not alter the fact that the distance between the old relationships and the new has been extended from both ends. There is also a similar "distance" between the old attitudes toward social work and public welfare, wholesomely rural, undeveloped and uninterpreted, and the new demands made by changed conditions. Growing out of these there will appear at once contrasts between the city and the county-wide situation. What problems and cases, due primarily to maladjustments in the city, belong primarily to the city? What problems carry over into the county? Which problems, therefore, should be handled through private and voluntary agencies and which through public welfare? What sort of organizations, therefore, should be provided for public welfare and what for voluntary groups? In the city itself, to what extent should a department of public welfare function, and what should be its relation to the private groups?

*Problems of Conflict.* It is inevitable, too, that conflict of opinions, conflict of groups, partisan interests and politics, as well as personal jealousies and rivalries, will play an important part in the early stages of development. It is not only the conflict of old ideas and ideals, but of old customs and procedure with those of different types; of old inhabitants with the new citizens; of old organizations striving to hold their own with, or dominate, those of the new order. Sometimes the conflict is on the issue of politics, sometimes religion, sometimes race, sometimes economic policies, sometimes sectional issues, and sometimes personalities. If the city be one of mining or industrial development, there are the contingencies arising out of capital and labor situations, while in other places various problems of political and social justice arise. And alongside all these are the difficulties of adjusting taxes and financial procedure of government to emergency situations.

*Of Direct and Indirect Importance.* These problems of social conflict are in themselves of great importance to the community. Their special significance, however, in this discussion is found in the difficulties which they engender in the whole problem of initiating, organizing, and administering social work and public welfare. Community organization, at best a difficult problem, becomes a seemingly impossible task under conditions of such conflicting currents and paradoxical alignments. And yet this situation of the rapid urbanization of American civilization is at once one of the most characteristic American phenomena, and one in which we apparently take greatest pride. Such problem cities, therefore, offer the greatest of opportunities for the development of their social interests in ways commensurate with their material development. They also challenge the whole profession of social work to see whether it can meet situations that are out of the usual, yet evolving into normal problems through their temporary abnormality. In the challenge is found the justification for our modern programs of social work and public welfare. To face the fact that at this present time our programs and social sciences are not big enough to meet the situation is a next step in the hopeful development of the whole field of social engineering. That it will require the best of the American spirit, of the spirit of Christian democracy, and of scientific standards there can be no doubt.

*The Scope of Problems to be Met.* Here, for instance, are cases of 194 families which have come to the attention of a small city within a month. One hundred and fifty-three of these were listed as major problems. These cases are of such variety

that their proper adjustments tax the whole
resources and best efforts of a community.  Eight
cases were feebleminded, fourteen represented
family desertions, six epileptics, forty-three handicapped, sixty-two ill, four insane, six criminals,
thirty-six with organic diseases, five with social
diseases, twelve homeless, and fifteen unemployed.
In the case of the families in trouble, seventy-
nine families assisted represented not widows or
broken homes, but married folks in trouble.
There were twenty-six widows, and twenty-five
separations.  In this group of families there were
324 adults assisted in some way or other and 309
children.  There were a number of cases where
individuals had come from other states and other
counties.  There were a number of expectant
mothers in trouble and a number of unmarried
and deserted mothers.  There were families all
members of which were below normal mentally.
There were families of four, five, and six, all ill in
one room.  There were examples where the co-
operation of the county commissioners, juvenile
court, county superintendent of public welfare,
and other governmental agencies were enlisted.
In all of these cases many visits, calls, and inter-
views as well as letters and conferences with
individuals and departments were necessary.

Here, then, are the problems and their challenge. How shall they be classified? Through what old and new organizations shall the community work? What is the best way to coördinate public and private work? How coördinate public welfare, public education, public health? How even pioneer through these difficult situations into new and better ways? How group these problems and work them out according to the best standards? How classify the remedial and curative efforts, and how plan for constructive and preventive programs in which will be included joint programs of education, health, community organization, and general social work?

*Remedial and Curative Efforts.* The first task of the cities will be found in attempting to meet and cope with all manner of maladjustment, suddenly come to their attention, as illustrated above, for which they must find cures. Later they will search after preventive and constructive measures. For the present their burdens of emergency tasks are heavy. This does not mean, of course, that in their efforts to meet emergency relief work of various sorts the best methods of social work will not be used, or that all possible preventive methods will not be utilized. But it does mean that the first group of problems will be those relating to relief, as found in the old terminology of charity and corrections. These problems are usually classified around three main divisions,—the *dependent folk*, the *delinquent folk,* and the *defective folk*. Such a classification cannot in the nature of the case be accurate. The groups overlap in many ways, in treatment, in causes, and in effects. The Children's Bureau at Washington, for instance, has just reported that of ten thousand delinquent youths studied, the majority of them begin with dependency or defectiveness in the home and surroundings. Many other illustrations will appear in the following analyses. The dependent or broken family may be the result of crime and neglect; the broken body, the blind child, the sick mother, and many other defectives and sick folks may find their first misfortune in delinquency or other mixed causes. This classification, therefore, is used merely as a basis for the analysis of problems and standards, and for conformity to other approaches to their study.

*Dependent Folks.* These are they who for various reasons are thrown upon society through some failure of social adjustment. They are not sufficient unto themselves. Their resources are inadequate. Their friends and relatives are unable to help them. The little children, the aged infirm, the broken families, the mothers with their families to be nurtured and educated, the transient wanderers whose paths have fallen in unguarded places, are considered. Society has somewhere failed them in their hour of need; and they in turn have failed society. What they need is adjustment and opportunity. They are lost, misplaced, misfits in the game of life. They want opportunity, help, understanding, not charity. In the treatment of all these cases the spirit of public welfare is that of democratic opportunity, of service rendered to these citizens as a part of the principle of equal opportunity. In the methods of assistance and social work the ideals are toward adjustment, the elimination of causes, the planning for the future. Above all, there must be help, not as charity or pauperizing influence, but help to help oneself. And it must be remembered that equal opportunity in the field of misfortune is no more charity than in the field of education, it is obligation. Society's unfortunates, therefore, become society's children, society's clients, for whom the best methods must be employed. And it is to the credit of society and

government that scientific and humane methods
have been worked out for each of the several
classes of dependent folk.

*Dependent Children.*   Little children left adrift
through no fault of their own, pupils of misfortune,
citizens of tomorrow—these constitute the first
group.   The fatherless, the motherless, the or-
phaned, the products of broken homes and families
—how shall they be provided for?   They need
opportunity, through wholesome surroundings
and direction, for normal life, happiness, and
purpose.   They need nurture, health, education,
work, play, worship, affection, growth.   How
shall they get it?   Through provisions for growing up under as nearly normal home and family
life conditions as possible.   The tendency is away
from the old institutional standards of grouping
large numbers of children together under forced
institutional atmosphere.   Whereas the old ideals
sought first an institutional home for the child,
the new plan seeks that last.   Through mothers'
aid, through community coöperation, through
child placing, the first effort is to keep the child in
its own home.   If this is not possible, the second
is to find it a good home, while the last is to send
it to an institution.   But even so, many must go

to institutions. Some must remain awhile until homes are found; some must remain for many years. The ideals, therefore, for the children's homes are that they conform as nearly as possible to normal homes, in their atmosphere, their general administration and arrangement, and in their educational efforts. Smaller units, well trained matrons, teachers, social workers, freedom and play, normal control and discipline, with no commercialization of childhood—these are the prevailing institutional standards.

A good statement of standards and ideals of child welfare, as expressed in the mothers' aid movement, is that of Miss Mary Bogue, director of Mothers' Assistance Fund in Pennsylvania and quoted by Miss Emeth Tuttle in her valuable manual on Mothers' Aid.

Our goal is the development of the personality and character of the children under our care; we believe that the family is the natural cradle wherein the adequate growth of human beings may be best fulfilled; and we discover that development within the framework of the family is dependent upon the proper functioning of the growing child in relation to six fundamental factors: health, education, work, recreation, worship, and beauty. Each of the elements of normal living must correlate in some kind of rhythmic fashion to render life harmonious and significant; and it is our duty to aid these children to function wholesomely on all six planes, for if one of these six elements be missing, the child's future will be crippled and distorted.

*Dependent Aged and Infirm.* The care of the older people who are left dependent upon the community usually involves two types of relief, outdoor and indoor. In each of these very definite advances have been made, and very definite standards set up, so that it looks entirely probable that this age-long dread of dependent old age may soon be mitigated. One of the best summaries of ideals and standards in this field is that just given by the Pennsylvania Department of Welfare.

(1) Make the county the unit of poor relief administration and abolish the township and borough systems.

(2) Create adequate provisions in the almshouse equipment for the present-day type of immates—the chronically ill and infirm. This means that the farming side of our almshouse administration must become subordinate entirely to that of properly taking care of the inmates and that the almshouse must be "hospitalized." Upon admission to the almshouse there should be a thorough medical examination of the inmates for proper classification and treatment.

(3) The poor boards must be made to realize that

outdoor relief should not be mere almsgiving through an endless chain of grocery orders, but that they should employ paid, full-time welfare workers to do constructive family case work.

The poor-directors' knowledge of the local neighborhood is of value in supplementing the results of systematic investigations, but we cannot expect the directors, who give only part time, to do the whole job, keeping in constant touch with all the families in their charge.

It is absolutely essential that there be close coöperation between the official poor-board and private charitable agencies, if the best results are to be obtained.

(4) We must realize that even if the county unit type of administration prevails in all our counties, some of the less populous counties do not have the resources to maintain the modern hospitalized county home. Where such conditions prevail every effort should be made to have the smaller counties join forces and thus establish a more effective and economical poor relief administration.

(5) Finally, there should be clearer recognition of the fact that there is a close relation between dependency and unemployment, industrial accidents and occupational diseases, and careful inquiry should be conducted to determine more accurately the proper methods for the alleviation of this "industrial dependency."

*Broken Homes*. Recent statistics estimate that one marriage out of every seven in the United States is dissolved by divorce, while it is estimated that as many more families are disorganized

by desertion, separation, and other causes.  This
would seem to indicate that about one-third of
the family life in this country is not stable.  Add
to this group industrial accidents, sickness, and
other providential handicaps, and one begins to
see something of the size of the relief problem
involved in broken homes and families.  In many
of these there is needed temporary relief, guidance,
and encouragement.  In many others some forms
of permanent relief and planning are required.
Here, again, great progress has been made in the
development of high standards and good social
methods.  This is primarily the field of social or
family case work, of which the main principles are
the adjustment of the family and its members to
normal living through directed planning, human
sympathy, and scientific methods.  One of the
most potent of influences here is that of  mothers'
aid already referred to.  Another is the wise administration of outdoor relief based upon recommendations of careful family case work.  Other
methods include the work of probation officers,
of domestic relation's courts, of community organization and neighborhood fellowship.  The difference between improper methods and proper
methods in this field not only involves elimina-

tion of tragedy and misfortune and failures, but also a great reduction in the economic cost to the people of city and county. The standards already quoted with reference to outdoor and indoor relief and with reference to mothers' aid in needy families will apply to these cases of broken homes. Other elements relating to legal and economic aspects of the situation will be discussed under the heading of the juvenile court and domestic relations.

*Homeless and Workless Folk.* In the rapidly growing city, with its influx of new citizens, workers, investors, adventurers, and the other types of transients, the man and woman without home and work, although not entirely or permanently dependent, will for sometime furnish one of the most urgent problems of relief. They, too, need adjustment, direction, opportunity, and sympathy. Least of all, they need sentimental charity and undirected assistance. The same high standards of case work and relief should be employed with transient individuals and groups as with all others. In addition, however, to the usual problems they involve also problems of intercommunity relationships, expenses for investigation and communication, relationship with other counties, cities and states in reciprocal, mutual aid, and wise direction and utilization of "back home" resources. For taking care of this burden the voluntary resources of a city should share the greater responsibility. The community chest or the combined and correlated efforts of such organizations as the Travellers' Aid Society, the Salvation Army, the Y. M. C. A., the Y. W. C. A., the Bureau of Family Welfare, or some branch of some work equivalent to the associated charities may all contribute to the solution of these problems and lighten the burden of the taxpayer in city and county. In this group, too, will be found many mothers who have not lived in the county or state long enough to receive mothers' aid. The problem here is to work out temporary relief through equitable coöperation between city and county, between voluntary and public agencies, so that temporary distress may not result in permanent dependency.

*Delinquent Folk.* The problem of the offender against law and society has always been one of the most difficult social problems with which communities must cope. In these new cities with new adjustments and with the consequent factors of dependency and conflict this problem becomes acute both in its quantitative aspects and in its treatment. Taken in consideration with the larger "crime wave" and lawlessness which is now being so much deplored, this problem of the delinquent becomes at once timely and urgent. Here again unusual advances have been made in the prevention and treatment of crime and delinquency. In the case of the juvenile offenders the standards and ideals involved in the juvenile court and probation work are very definite. Likewise, in the administration of prisons and prison camps and chain gangs there have been wholesome advances in methods. These will be analyzed briefly in subsequent paragraphs. There are, however, certain general ideals and standards with reference to crime and criminals which show marked progress. The old principle of "an eye for an eye" is no longer the chief motive of punishment. Punishment of the individual, methods for redeeming the individual and saving him from utter ruin and for future citizenship, and the protection of society make the threefold basis upon which effective programs must be organized. Other ideals involving humane treatment of prisoners and scientific approach to the whole subject are important

developments. Growing out of these modern
methods, however, are still other problems and
dangers relating to the passing of too many laws,
confusing of major offenses with minor offenses,
long delays in trials, and the making of punishment inadequate.

*The Juvenile Court.* As in the case of the dependent folk, the first group which demands attention is that of youth. There is, of course, the
potential of the offender in every child. Society's
objective is to turn the child into the strong individual, and to prevent him from becoming weak
and delinquent. And there are many factors,
many variations, much difference in individuals,
and many aspects of mental and social irregular-
ity to be taken into consideration. The child
and youth offender is no longer herded with hard-
ened criminals. He is no longer treated like the
seasoned criminal. The preventive aspects are
emphasized more and more. For the remedial part
of juvenile delinquency the juvenile court represents the modern advance. For the preventive
work the juvenile court and community agencies
of recreation and leisure time activities provide
the hopeful programs. One of the best summaries of the ideals and standards of the juvenile

court is that just given by the Children's Bureau of the Department of Labor at Washington.

Lack of understanding and sympathy at home may explain the stubborn child who feels himself alone in the world, and, like pirate craft, defies the standards of the group. Erratic and inconsistent treatment at home, based on the whim and caprice of father or mother, is reflected in the sullen and unruly child who neither understands discipline nor respects law. The untruthful child may be imitating the morals he has observed practised, rather than those he hears preached. The child who steals may do so because his parents have low standards, because of a love of adventure, because his "gang" does so, or perhaps because he is hungry or cold. The truant may be the victim of bad adjustment at school. In all these cases the task of the juvenile court is to study the family, home, and school, to help parents and teachers to understand the child, and to provide a safe outlet for the energies which have flowed through destructive channels. Love of adventure, to take one example, may be harnessed to give us the explorer, the inventor, the pioneer, instead of the thief, or the wanderer. The gang spirit may, if properly directed, give us boy and girl scouts; baseball games may use constructively the energy which threatens to tear down; a sympathetic "big brother" or "big sister" may melt the stubborn heart of the child to whom the world has seemed full of enemies and injustice.

To make our juvenile courts serve their end—for saving, not punishing, the child—the community must see that the court has enough money to provide experienced and sympathetic probation officers and social workers; that there is a good clinic connected with the court where the child's physical and mental defects may be studied and remedied; that the law permits the judge to deal with the child informally and individually.

The policeman's club, the patrol wagon, the formal atmosphere of the adult court, have no place in dealing with children. The delinquent child is a sick child. The business of the children's court is to see that he is made well morally, socially, and perhaps even physically. Wisdom, patience, and love are the weapons which must replace the "big stick."

Two questions for you and your community: Have you a juvenile court? Is it properly equipped to save children?

*Prisons and Jails.* With the procedure of the law and with court machinery this volume is not primarily concerned, however important they may be. It is concerned, however, with the means and methods of dealing with offenders themselves, as one of the most important phases of public welfare. The offender or criminal is a client of government, and whatever social work is done for his benefit must come, directly or indirectly, through the channel of public welfare. There are many important principles involved, in addition to the general ideals already stated, as applying to crime and criminals in general. There is the problem of the offender's family, for which provision must be made. There are the problems of mental, physical, and social health, in which every care should be exercised to understand the situation, to give the offender the right treatment, and to protect the community against him, or to restore him to the community. The criminal is often a sick man, sick in body, in mind, and spirit. Therefore, he needs special attention. He is, it is true, a violator of law and community standards; consequently his freedom is taken away. It is important, however, that he be not treated as a slave or with cruelty or inhumane methods. Thus the new standard for prisons and jails has tended to make possible much better social treatment and cures than the old standards. In the local jails it is fairly easy to set down good standards; it is not easy to bring them to pass. Among the minimum standards are the following: safety and security, health giving and sanitary surroundings, reasonable treatment and comfort, separation of the sexes, separation of youth from maturity, segregation of the diseased, proper utilization of prisoner's time, proper mental and physical examinations, the elimination of politics as far as possible, and the economic and efficient administration of the whole prison system. It may often happen that a single county or town may not seem able to uphold such standards without coöperating with other towns, counties, or districts to maintain joint units of control. For state-wide and Federal units there are other important principles involved. The employment of prisoners on farms, in industries, and inside the institutions themselves constitutes one of the most important aspects. The ideal would tend toward the standards already mentioned for local prisons, and in addition toward partial maintenance, toward partial support by prisoners of the family back home, toward educational and corrective measures, including vocational guidance and direction, and physical rejuvenation. Involved are also the important problems of probation and parole, as well as financial aspects such as centralized buying of supplies and selling of products, and questions of state control and supervision. Reasonable supervision of all institutions, rather than autocratic control, is the accepted best standard.

*The County Chain Gang.* The task of keeping county prisoners busy, as well as that of housing those whose sentences range over several months or longer is a difficult one. In the South the chain gang has been utilized for this purpose and has perhaps caused more criticism than any other phase of prison administration. Charges of cruelty, of inhumane treatment, of peonage, and even of murder have been broadcast throughout the nation. The problem has been further complicated by the presence of large numbers of negroes as well as whites, and the consequent necessary dual system of housing and work. The traditional attitude of the Southerner of less liberal experience and training has accentuated the seriousness of the situation. Everywhere admitted to be one of the most difficult of problems, the chain gang has challenged the South to better efforts and standards. Here is a distinct problem of public welfare which needs effective standards. Some of the principles involved include:

> Integral and wholesome coördination with all other public welfare and county government units.
>
> Economic and efficient administration of all phases of administration.
>
> Effective and humane supervision and control of prisoners.
>
> Sanitary and healthful camps and surroundings.

Physical and medical examination, treatment and segregation of prisoners when necessary.

Work on county and state projects rather than lease to private concerns.

Like the county jail and the county home, it may be advisable for counties to join efforts in district units from time to time.[2]

*The Defective and Crippled Folk.* The third great class of the socially deficient is that which consists of those whose minds and bodies are defective or broken. In this group, too, are the little children; the crippled and broken bodies but normal minds; the blind, deaf and dumb; the insane, the feeble-minded, the morons and the idiots, at once a tragedy and a menace. We have already referred to the aged infirm in the county homes. In this group are also the mature folk, blind, broken, handicapped for life, some congenitally, some accidentally. In this group are the most poignant tragedies of the social order. Here again have developed high standards and ideals, and saner attitudes of treatment. In these groups, however, is involved much that is technical in the field of medicine, psychiatry, law,

[2] See questions for study at the end of this chapter.

and eugenics. The problem of treatment becomes more nearly a state-wide problem than a local one. Thus the local community and county contribute their part to the upkeep and maintenance of their quota, either in their own domain or in larger units. Here also are the important contributions of churches and varied voluntary groups. Of particular importance are the newer ideals which respect the sick in mind as well as body, and which recognize the danger of the abnormal to normal society. Important, too, are the raised institutional standards of treatment, the great advances in educational methods, and the facilities and disposition to make proper use of the leisure time of such unfortunates.

*Preventive and Constructive Measures.* When a community has given temporary relief to its distressed individuals and groups it has but begun its larger program of social adjustment. While emergency relief is absolutely essential, and in a given emergency is more important than anything else at the time, it is of secondary importance for the public good in the long run. What is needed is prevention of social deficiency and development of the normal life. It has already been pointed out how mothers' aid may become the ounce of prevention which may save pounds of misery and suffering. It has been pointed out how the juvenile court and the new methods of treating youthful offenders may save for society thousands of youth who might be lost. It has been pointed out, too, how effective family case work and good social work methods in the treatment of the offender, the homeless and workless man, and others may be used in constructive ways. But in addition to this, the community must be on the lookout always for the constructive work through which it may reduce its relief problem and its abnormality, and through which it may increase its prosperity, happiness, and normality. In this field will be found the varied programs of recreation and education for the proper use of leisure time. Here will be problems of the supervision of commercial recreation, and of the planning of community organizations. Here are problems of the school as community centers, of church, of civic agencies and of service groups throughout the community. Here are problems of the Y. M. C. A. and Y. W. C. A., of the Travellers' Aid, of the Red Cross, and of those other agencies which go to make up the total of a community council of social work agencies. Here are problems of the wise utilization and coördination of medical, educational, and public welfare science and methods. Here are distinctive problems for each of the three groups to work out. The county government must look to its constructive programs within its department of public welfare, the city government must not neglect its playgrounds, parks, and recreation programs, and the voluntary agencies must not forget their part in the whole preventive program.

*First Essentials.* From the foregoing analysis of the situations and problems facing the rapidly growing city and the county in which it is located there appear certain fairly clear-cut conclusions. The first one is that it is absolutely necessary to provide leaders and workers of strong personality, good training, and adequate experience to deal with these problems. It must be clear to anyone that no board of citizens or administrative lay group, busy with other affairs and untrained in the special field, can either understand these problems or work them out. It must be clear, too, that the same sort of high class specialists are needed in the field of public welfare and social work as are already used with great success in the fields of education, of health, of law, of engineering, of business, and the other fundamental phases of progress. Such leaders and social workers will not only help work out standards and give guidance to community, but will become the responsible agents for administrative groups.

*Continuity of Plan and Personality.* Another essential that seems absolutely clear, although usually overlooked in the field of public welfare and social work, is the continuity of plan and personnel from year to year. At best, social work and public welfare show results slowly and require hard work and much experiment to yield final results. It is absolutely necessary, therefore, that there be devised county systems and city systems of public welfare, so organized in connection with other aspects of government as to insure regularity and continuity of departmental efforts from year to year. Such a plan will, of course, tend to encourage continuity of personality as opposed to the changing of social workers according to the whim of individual groups and of individual situations. One of the greatest handicaps in the whole field of social work is the high percentage of labor turnover, and the common consciousness among citizens that the work may be stopped at any time when it suits the whims or convenience of particular groups.

*Patience and Persistence.* A commonplace but important conclusion is that this problem of finding leaders, of working out statute and technique in new fields requires unusual patience and persistence. There are, in the first place, relatively few big leaders and technicians in this field. This is but natural for the simple reason that it is a new field which has not found its full place in the scheme of government and community. It is literally, therefore, impossible to expect perfect results in the beginning. The ideal will be to approximate the best results with the best leaders available, but with always the goal in view of developing present leaders and of training new ones. This is true not only in the field of public welfare, but in the whole field of social work where hundreds of special workers fail because of their inability to adapt themselves to situations and needs, and because of a lack of community consciousness and programs. Not only are there not leaders enough, but the field is new and there are many difficulties to be worked out in the task of having the government take its due part in social relief and adjustment. It is better to begin with those things which can be done well, and to develop as rapidly as possible the whole program. Mistakes will be made, and the tendency will be to condemn the whole field for mistakes in a part of it. It should be remembered, however, that this has been true in education and public health and all other fields of social endeavor. No one wishes to eliminate the public school system because of its blunders and limitations. Why, therefore, decry the whole field of public welfare because of its newness and imperfections? To do so is to despair of the whole democratic processes of social development.

*Coöperation and Coördination of Efforts.* In all community work coöperative effort is, of course, a basic necessity. In the field of public welfare, co-operation lies at the very heart of all success. So many of the problems involve varying disciplines and specialities. The delinquent boy may need the coöperative effort of the school folks, of school attendance officer, of probation officer, of the juvenile court, of the family case worker, of the physician, of the psychiatrist, of the public health nurse, of the church, of the boy scout agency, and others. In such a coöperative program, it is easy to see that there may be involved the county superintendent of public welfare, the juvenile court judge, the probation officer, the city or public welfare department, and varied private agencies. Thus, whereas in other departments of government coöperation is highly desirable, in public welfare it is absolutely essential. There is, then, the very necessary coöperation between private agencies and public effort, and coöperation between personalities, strong, striking, and militant in their special fields of work.

*Governmental Responsibility for Social Work.* Because of the importance of public welfare and social work to modern society, and because of the complexity of problems and relationships, there is first of all, therefore, need of definiteness in organization and skill in legislation. Without doubt, the first essential is to provide in county, city, and state, governmental systems of public welfare which are as adequate, as definite, and as effective as other phases of government, such as public education, public health, good roads, and finances. In Chapters I and VIII of this volume some of the principles involved in public welfare have been discussed. In a previous volume, *Systems of Public Welfare*, certain definitions and principles have been set forth, showing the importance of public welfare as that part of government which has for its chief emphasis the making

of democracy effective in the unequal places.    The
next task is to work out simple, practical, and con-
sistent units of public welfare in county, city, and
state, and to establish this principle and practice
once and for all in the realm of American government.

*Voluntary Responsibility for Social Work.*    There
are, nevertheless, as in other social efforts, many
problems and phases of social work and experiment which can best be done by voluntary groups
and agencies.    In the concrete example cited
above, for instance, of the 179 cases, which came to
the attention of the city department of public welfare within a month, the great majority came from
families who had not been permanent residents of
the city.    Most of these, for instance, were not
eligible for mothers' aid and other governmental
assistance.    Many of them were brought there by
industry and economic development, and much of
the relief needed by them should be borne by those
who are profiting by the growth of the city.    Many
cases are mere transients and should not in any
wise be the burden of a county-wide program.
Many cases involve moral and religious direction.
It is very clear that many of these cases should
find relief through means and measures not avail-

able to county or city government. Other functions of the private agencies are to experiment and to blaze trails which later may be taken up and perfected by government if proved good. Other functions of private agencies are to stimulate, to check, to coöperate with, governmental public welfare. Other functions are those of developing interest in citizens, of training for citizenship, of utilizing lay voluntary activities, and of developing the whole field of community organization and Christian coöperation.

*A Three-fold Organization Program.* The conclusion would seem warranted, therefore, that three distinct types of organization are necessary in such cities as have been described. There is the county-wide department of public welfare with its responsible and well trained head upon whom will devolve the responsibility of governmental social work for the county. This means, of course, all of the phases of deficiencies and remedial efforts which have been described. Whatever of expert technique and scientific methods are needed must be worked out through this department, which must be responsible to county officials. There is, then, also necessary a city department of public welfare organized directly under the city manager

or other forces of city government with the same
general standards and ideals outlined for the
county department. Such a department will include the programs for relief and also for recreation and constructive measures. There is, then,
the third essential which will include all voluntary
community organizations for social work. The
number and nature of these organizations will vary
considerably according to the needs and history
of the city and county. But, in general, there will
be needed two larger coördinating organizations.
The one will have for its purpose the raising of
finances, while the other will have for its purposes
the coördination of effort and the limitation of
duplication and inefficiency. The first type is
usually some form of community chest, while the
second takes the form of a community council of
social agencies. Sometimes it is a welfare federation, sometimes it is city-wide and sometimes it is
county-wide. Such a three-fold organization, well
planned, ought to go far toward successful community work.

SPECIAL QUESTIONS FOR STUDY AND ILLUSTRATIONS

XXXVI. *Public Health and Public Welfare.* In
the different cities problems of social
hygiene, of health, and public welfare

are so related that there is a growing tendency to recommend that the department of public welfare in the city shall include relief, constructive social planning, and many of the public health problems.

Point out items in favor of this arrangement and against it.

XXXVII. *Selection of the County Public Welfare Official.* Since so many of the problems of public welfare in the county are closely related to the school system and to school attendance work, there are many who believe that the public welfare officials should be chosen jointly by the county commissioners and the county board of education. This is true in North Carolina.

Point out advantages and disadvantages in this plan.

XXXVIII. *Selection by a County Council or Board.* There are many students of this problem who feel that if the public welfare official is selected solely by a limited number of county officials there may be the usual danger of political appointment. Various suggestions are made. One is the Virginia plan whereby a county board of public welfare previously selected and appointed with due authority will elect the officer. Others recommend that a county-wide voluntary council appoint such an officer.

Point out in this last plan the dangers to democratic government and the general objections involved.

XXXIX. *Regional County Homes.* In both North Carolina and Virginia the state departments of public welfare think the rural county is often too small a unit for the support of an almshouse, and both favor the establishment of district homes or hospitals. Indiana, on the other hand, has developed what is recognized as one of the most efficient systems of outdoor relief in this country, using the township as the unit.

Give evidence in favor of the regional county home.

XL. *State-wide Supervision of Prisoners.* A student of prisons and prison conditions has the following to say: "I do not believe that there will ever be anything approaching scientific or even decently efficient treatment of prisoners on the county unit basis. The one idea is and will continue to be the exploitation of the labor of the prisoner. The cost of anything approaching the needed classification and segregation of prisoners in the county is prohibitive. The only hope of a solution of the problem of the offender, I believe, if there be any possible solution, is in state control of all prisoners. The voluntary district of small counties might be an improvement, but there are so many practical difficulties as to make such a plan impossible."

Discuss this opinion.

XLI. *County and City Coöperation.* In matters of prisons, roads, finances, and other things, counties, cities, and states have worked out very definite and satisfactory plans of coöperation and distribution of efforts. Public welfare involves similar problems, with perhaps even more complication.

Sketch out a plan whereby there may be equitable distribution of efforts between city, county, and state in certain definite problems of public welfare.

# CHAPTER X

## A SUGGESTED DISTRIBUTION OF ASSIGNMENTS

Since this outline may be adapted to very elementary work or more comprehensive study, methods of using it must necessarily vary greatly. In the classroom, for instance, it may be often wise to omit entirely Chapter III, dealing with social problems, for the reason that a separate course using other texts may be desired. In such case an entirely different assignment of topics will be necessary. The suggested arrangement which follows, therefore, is offered simply to indicate one way of dividing the study so that it will insure completion within given periods. Even for county superintendents of public welfare and others who do not wish college or extension credit, it is often wise to take the book up systematically and work it out by topics.

In answering questions, emphasis should be placed on concreteness, definiteness, and accuracy rather than long or wordy discussions. In a course of this sort what is most desired for this approach to public welfare and social work is a simple clear-cut understanding of the problems and situations studied. Practise in summarizing information and in writing it down briefly and concisely will prove to be one of the chief values of the course. Checking one's knowledge definitely rather than assuming in general that in all probability one knows the subject will also prove a profitable exercise.

Questions in the volume are numbered consecutively from one to 393, irrespective of chapters, so that references to or discussions of any given questions may be thereby facilitated.

In the same way topics and questions for discussion and illustration are numbered from I to XLI. In this group of topics ample opportunity is given for more elaborate illustration, description, originality of presentation and general discussion. Equally important, alongside the questions which demand accurate and concrete factual replies, are opportunities for making application, illustration, and plans. In some ways, therefore, the topics for illustration will be tests of the effectiveness with which the student has gained information in the previous parts of the book.

The study of the volume, finally, is divided

into three main divisions; the first is the text matter presented by the author in all of chapters I, VIII, and IX together with introductory paragraphs to each of the subjects studied in all other chapters. The second important division of study is that based directly upon the several reference texts as listed below and as specified in each chapter in its proper place. The third division of study is that represented by the topics in Roman numerals, in which the student is expected to know the subject well enough and to concentrate upon his problem well enough to make effective applications to his own field of public welfare and social work.

The minimum requirements in reference texts for the course will be:

*The Equipment of the Social Worker*, by Macadam, Henry Holt and Company, New York.
*Problems of Citizenship*, by Baker-Crothers and Hudnut, Henry Holt and Company, New York.
*Social Pathology*, by Queen, Lippincott, Philadelphia.
*Problems of Child Welfare*, by Mangold, The Macmillan Company, New York.
*The Human Factor in Industry*, by Frankel

and Fleisher, The Macmillan Company, New York.

*The Challenge of the Country*, by Fiske, The Association Press, New York.

*Community Organization*, by Steiner, The Century Company, New York.

Supplementary reference books which may be used for more extended study will include:

*Systems of Public Welfare*, by Odum and Willard, University of North Carolina Press, Chapel Hill.

*Education and Training for Social Work*, by Tufts, Russell Sage Foundation, New York.

*Education of Social Work*, by Steiner, University of Chicago Press, Chicago.

*The Art of Helping People Out of Trouble*, by De Schweinitz, Houghton Mifflin Company, Boston.

### FIRST ASSIGNMENT

*Chapter I*

Give a half dozen concepts or ideas of "public welfare."

Give a half dozen concepts or ideas of "social work."

Write out your own definition of each.

Illustrate with a half dozen instances the importance of social work methods in public welfare activities.

Why is it that the college professor and many of the highest educated individuals among the professions are unsympathetic with public welfare and social work?

Which is the greater obstacle to the development of social work and public welfare standards, the common man who misunderstands the spirit and method or the college professor and politician who satirizes the whole field?

SECOND ASSIGNMENT

*Chapter II*
Answer questions 1 to 6.
Illustrate Topics I and II.

THIRD ASSIGNMENT

*Chapter II*
Answer questions 7 to 19.
Illustrate Topic III.

FOURTH ASSIGNMENT

*Chapter II*
Answer questions 20 to 32.
Illustrate Topic IV.

FIFTH ASSIGNMENT

*Chapter II*
Answer questions 36 to 40.
Illustrate Topics V and VI.

SIXTH ASSIGNMENT

*Chapter III*
Answer questions 43 to 55.
Illustrate Topic VII.

SEVENTH ASSIGNMENT

*Chapter III*
Answer questions 56 to 63.
Illustrate Topic VIII.

EIGHTH ASSIGNMENT

*Chapter III*
Answer questions 64 to 75.
Illustrate Topic IX.

NINTH ASSIGNMENT

*Chapter III*
Answer questions 76 to 90.
Illustrate Topic X.

TENTH ASSIGNMENT

*Chapter IV*
Answer questions 91 to 101.
Illustrate Topic XI.

ELEVENTH ASSIGNMENT

*Chapter IV*
Answer questions 102 to 114.
Illustrate Topic XII.

TWELFTH ASSIGNMENT

*Chapter IV*
Answer questions 115 to 126.
Illustrate Topic XIII.

THIRTEENTH ASSIGNMENT

*Chapter IV*
Answer questions 143 to 156.
Illustrate Topics XIV and XV.

FOURTEENTH ASSIGNMENT

*Chapter V*
Answer questions 159 to 177.
Illustrate Topic XVI.

FIFTEENTH ASSIGNMENT

*Chapter V*
Answer questions 178 to 191.
Illustrate Topic XVII.

SIXTEENTH ASSIGNMENT

*Chapter V*
Answer questions 192 to 203.
Illustrate Topic XVIII.

SEVENTEENTH ASSIGNMENT

*Chapter V*
Answer questions 204 to 210.
Illustrate Topic XIX.

### EIGHTEENTH ASSIGNMENT

*Chapter V*
Answer questions 211 to 219.
Illustrate Topic **XX**.

### NINETEENTH ASSIGNMENT

*Chapter V*
Answer questions 220 to 234.
Illustrate wrong placement of children in an institution.

### TWENTIETH ASSIGNMENT

*Chapter VI*
Answer questions 235 to 251.
Illustrate Topic **XXI**.

### TWENTY-FIRST ASSIGNMENT

*Chapter VI*
Answer questions 252 to 275.
Illustrate Topic **XXII**.

### TWENTY-SECOND ASSIGNMENT

*Chapter VI*
Answer questions 282 to 299.
Describe experiments in industrial democracy.

### TWENTY-THIRD ASSIGNMENT

*Chapter VI*
Answer questions 300 to 318.
Illustrate Topic **XXIII**.

TWENTY-FOURTH ASSIGNMENT

*Chapter VII*
Answer questions 325 to 338.
Illustrate Topic **XXIV**.

TWENTY-FIFTH ASSIGNMENT

*Chapter VII*
Answer questions 339 to 348.
Illustrate Topic **XXV**.

TWENTY-SIXTH ASSIGNMENT

*Chapter VI*
Answer questions 349 to 368.
Illustrate Topic **XXVI**.

TWENTY-SEVENTH ASSIGNMENT

*Chapter VII*
Answer questions 369 to 380.
Illustrate Topic **XXVII**.

TWENTY-EIGHTH ASSIGNMENT

*Chapter VII*
Answer questions 381 to 393.
Illustrate Topic **XXVIII**.

TWENTY-NINTH ASSIGNMENT

*Chapter VIII*
Illustrate Topics **XXIX, XXX, XXXI, XXXII**.

THIRTIETH ASSIGNMENT

*Chapter VIII*
Illustrate Topics XXXIII, XXXIV, XXXV.

THIRTY-FIRST ASSIGNMENT

*Chapter IX*
Illustrate   Topics   XXXVI,   XXXVII,
XXXVIII, XXXIX.

THIRTY-SECOND ASSIGNMENT

*Chapter IX*
Illustrate the situation described in Chapter IX.
Illustrate Topics XL, XLI.

www.ingramcontent.com/pod-product-compliance
Lightning Source LLC
Chambersburg PA
CBHW030651270326
41929CB00007B/305